About the

Harry Leslie Smith is a survivor o
world war RAF veteran and, at 90, an activist for the p
the preservation of social democracy. His Guardian articles have been
shared over 60,000 times on Facebook and have attracted huge
comment and debate. He has authored numerous books about
Britain during the Great Depression, the Second World War and
post-war austerity. He lives outside Toronto, Canada and in
Yorkshire.
Harry Leslie Smith books are represented by Greene & Heaton. His
latest book "Harry's Last Stand" is published by Icon and available
for sale in June 2014

To My Son Peter

1959-2009

The Empress of Australia:
A Post-War Memoir

Harry Leslie Smith

The Empress of Australia: A Post-War Memoir

Copyright: Harry Leslie Smith

Barley Hole Press
Sydney Street,
Belleville, Ontario, Canada
K8P 4Y1
www.1923thebook.ca

ISBN: 0987842579
ISBN: 9780987842572

Printed in the United States of America

v

Acknowledgements:

There are so many people I would like to thank for their assistance in completing this book and my two previous works. Firstly, I must thank my son John for insisting that the history of my early life was worthy enough that it should be preserved. His dogged devotion to me and to my writings has not only kept me sane through these so-called golden years, it has also given me the strength to carry on after the loss of my son Peter.

Roy, Irma, Paddy, Margaret, Dorothy, Eric, Ingrid, and Norman: thank you for sharing your friendship and the travails while we lived in post-war Britain.

Mickey and Betty: although you didn't figure prominently in this book, your friendship to me and Friede was profound.

Mickey: you were a brother to me, and I feel blessed that we met and were able to enjoy so many years of friendship

I cannot thank enough Mary Mallison, my cousin in Australia, for her exhaustive research into our family's early history. Nor can I forget my nephew Derek and wife Trish for their support. Margaret Elliott, I must also thank for encouraging me to continue writing, and my friend Melanie for doing the same.

Andrew Emery: thank you for not only being my physician, but my friend throughout all these years; may we enjoy many more glasses of wine together.

I would also like to thank my friend Haig Tootikian and his wife Anahis for their support and love over the years. I am a lucky man to have so many people in my life at so late a date.

"I don't care a damn about men who are loyal to the people who pay them, to organizations...I don't think even my country means all that much. There are many countries in our blood, aren't there, but only one person. Would the world be in the mess it is if we were loyal to love and not to countries?"
— *Graham Greene, Our Man in Havana*

Chapter One:
The Green and Pleasant Land

In the winter of 1948, a post-war darkness felled Britain, and happiness, like sweets, was tightly rationed. Dunkirk, The Battle of Britain, The Blitz, Normandy, and even Churchill's V for victory were now past. They were like points of light flickering in the night sky, distant and far away. These events were now part of our nation's proud history but they offered us few clues as to how we were to survive the Age of Austerity that followed the war.

For an ordinary bloke like me, it was hard to square either in my head or in my heart that peace yielded such a paltry dividend, especially after so much blood had been spilt to achieve it. The arithmetic just didn't add up. It didn't make sense to me that after years of bitter struggle, after immeasurable death and destruction were wrought upon our people and our homeland - all peace had to offer us was a "thank you very much."

For a lot of people, the beer started to grow stale not long after the articles of absolute surrender was signed and the troops were demobbed. Many believed that it was time that the Kingdom shared some of its wealth and power with those that had fought to defend the island during our dark struggle for survival. When the General Election was held in the summer of 1945, the people spoke and ushered Prime Minister Churchill and the Conservative Party out from the corridors of power.

The Labour Party was our new master of state. It was only natural because they had promised the lower ranks that their blood, sweat, and tears were worth something in this new world that was free of tyrants. Under Prime Minister Attlee, it was hoped that the citizens of Great Britain were about to witness a return to a green and pleasant land where a Jerusalem, if you will, was to be erected for all under her dominion.

Unfortunately for those that had fought the hardest and sacrificed the most, our country was on the verge of insolvency. Our nation resembled a dowager spinster who because of reduced circumstances and poor health clung to life in a work house hospital ward. We were haemorrhaging in red ink and past due notices, and our debts were not going to be forgiven or forgotten by those that had lent us the credit to combat evil. The cost of waging this war had gravely wounded us, and like Babylon, the Hittites, Athens, or Rome, the United Kingdom's empire was lost.

I knew that nothing was going to prevent Britain from tumbling to the ground. We'd had our chips. Britain's moment of greatness, like a January's twilight, had faded into the stratosphere. My country's majesty and antique splendour rested unquiet and resentful in the Elysian field reserved for once and former kingdoms. In 1948's cold and austere frost, my nation was as poor as a pauper living rough.

So despite revolutionary talk, from the green benches in the House of Commons, about giving the common man his due, I knew that if this was to happen; it was going to take as long as Moses' walk through the desert to the promised land. Nothing was going to change for the better for me or my kind as long as the nation's real power was held by the corporate mandarins of coal, wool, and steel along with London's grey men of finance. It was not in the interests of the moguls, the aristocrats or the royals to surrender their wealth to the masses to build an egalitarian society. No matter what bills or laws Labour were about to pass in the House, the ruling class were going to bitterly oppose it as they believed God himself had showered them with the right to rule us.

There was no way of getting around it: 1948 was not a good year for me and anyone else trying to get ahead in a society divided so efficiently between the have and the have not's. It was vinegar vintage for both young and old alike. If it had been my choice to make, the moment the clock towers from London to Edinburgh tolled the end for1947, I would have poured the New Year down the drain.

I suppose I should have been more optimistic about the forty-eighth year of the twentieth century. After all, I was about to turn twenty-five, and in a matter of months I was to be shorn free of my military duties. After the war ended, I had stayed on in the forces because I wasn't sure what to do with my life. The most reasonable option seemed to me was to stick with what I knew best, and that was being an A/C in the RAF. At least as a member of the Royal Air Force, I was guaranteed food and lodging while I got my own affairs in order.

2

I had been at his Majesty's beck and call since 1941, and I felt comfortable in the ranks and in my blue uniform. In many ways, it had been more of a family to me than my own. Nobody would have believed me if I told them that the safest I had ever felt in my life was as a member of the RAF. Perhaps some of that feeling of security had to do with the fact that I had what was known amongst veterans as a *good war*.

Outside of needing the odd plaster for a shaving cut, I had walked away from the clash of civilizations without injury. I was never asked to give my life, the ultimate sacrifice, to my nation. Had it been requested, I don't think I would have volunteered it without a great deal of deliberation and consideration. Fortunately for me the subject never came up and I was one of the lucky ones. I only had to remit to the nation my feet to march the length and breadth of the country, my lungs to roar like a lion when a sergeant- major beckoned, my right hand to salute officers, NCO's, big dogs and telephone poles when I had too much to drink. The final appendage I surrendered to them was my arse, which endured innumerable territorial manoeuvres across the country, in an antiquated Leyland Lorry.

It was only near the war's end that someone in the Air Ministry decided it was about bloody time that my squadron got its feet wet and we were packed off to Europe. We landed in Belgium and made our way to Holland before ending up in Hamburg Germany. Our task was to take control of liberated axis air fields and make them operational for the allied war effort. While in the theatre of conflict, no one in my BAFU unit came to any real harm except for the odd exception where drink, cards, money or a woman was involved.

There is no proper explanation as to why I outlived the war while millions of other young men and women became extinct. One thing was for certain: it had nothing to do with a divine grace. I was sure that if God existed, He'd be better at doing sums because it just didn't make sense for my worth to the cosmos to be greater in value than twenty million Russians, six million Jews, a million gypsies or fifty-five thousand lads in bomber command. So much love, laughter and potential was extinguished during the war, that it was evident to me that God or not God; He was of no bloody use to any of us mortals.

My survival, I reasoned was just the computations of a blind and amoral universe. Still, if a ripple in the solar wind disturbed a proton and bumped an atom and propelled good luck my way, I wasn't going to complain. Being alive and not being maimed after the rivers of Europe flowed with the blood of both the innocent and the guilty taught me that for most, life was all too brief and usually painfully unfair. I survived the war by random luck, but I knew that peace in post-war Britain was a different matter. There, the cards were definitely stacked against me because I had been born into an unhappy and desperately poor family.

Anyone who knew my parents and our early circumstances would agree that I started out life a tuppence short when it came to good fortune. Even my mother granted that I was buggered from the day I was born when it came to luck. Since we had so little of it, she advised me once to "Grab it while you can because for everyday of sunshine, there shall be three that piss upon thy head."

My mum held many incorrect opinions about the world, but I was willing to concede to her the wisdom in knowing that bad luck favours the poor. It was something that she understood all too well as we came from Yorkshire's harsh and unforgiving South and West Counties. It was a region abundant in coal mines, cotton mills, and work houses. T.B., rickets, and black lung trolled the dirty cramped slums and over populated terrace houses of my youth. As a boy, I had become all too familiar with the holy trinity for the poor: the rent collector, the money lender, and the bailiff.

I suppose it was only natural that after the war ended I wanted something better for myself than the hand-to-mouth existence of my parents. I didn't want anything extravagant; I simply believed I deserved more out of my time on this Earth than flogging my Sunday best at the pawn brokers because there was nothing to eat in the larder.

I wanted my post-war life to have élan and a touch of star dust, and I didn't think that was too much to ask considering that I had endured the Great Depression and survived the twentieth century's Second Great War. I was a young man that needed a purpose, but above all else I wanted to find someone to love. I wanted my life to have meaning, and I believed the only way it was worth living was with a woman who would return my affections with equal ardour. I hoped a kiss from my true love, a look, or an embrace from her might reveal to me the enigma of my existence.

Since I was an adolescent, I'd pursued love, but up until I was stationed in Hamburg, Germany, I'd never found my heart's equal. It was there I encountered a woman who became the greatest love of my life. She was a german named Elfriede Edelmann, and she was unique. She intrigued me, and I was smitten from the moment I set eyes upon her at a black market. I thought her rare personality and movie star good looks were created from magic rather than from her topsy-turvy home life. Eventually, we became lovers, and she inspired me to do great things with my limited talents.

At the beginning of our courtship, she loved me with the ambivalence of a woman jilted by the cruelty of the era we occupied. After the brutality of the Second World War, hesitant love was perhaps the most two people from opposing sides of the conflict could expect from each other.

She was known to her intimates as Friede, and to me as luv. For me, being in her company was like being in dazzling warm sunlight after a lifetime spent in a land of cold, winter rain. As I was dangerously infatuated by her, sometimes the light Friede cast upon me played tricks upon my eyes. I was like a moth to a flame, easily singed by her flickering glow. She besotted me and entranced me with her physical beauty, her style, and her individuality. But, it was her profound emotions and thoughts that trapped me for good. I was love struck and wanted her to be my life's companion.

Exactly what Friede made of me, her *Tommy boyfriend*, was more of an enigma. Some days I was her lover, on other occasions I was her provider, and sometimes I was just her friend and confidant. Living under Nazism had damaged her, like so many of Germany's children. It had warped the frame that encased her spirit. Friede was a strong enough person to recognize the harm done to her and admitted to me, "Because I grew up in the shadow of Hitler and the Nazis, my emotions are sometimes like hot and cold lava. At times I am nervous and afraid of the unknown because as a girl, I lived in a country where we feared the knock of the Gestapo against our door at midnight. The way I grew up makes me sometimes very suspicious about people and their true intent. Sometimes I am terrified for my future or what will become of both you and me."

5

I tried to calm her fears about me, about the world and about our future. But truthfully, I didn't understand the gravity of her apprehensions, until we married in August 1947. It had been a long fought ordeal to get approval for our nuptials but wedded life proved to be more formidable for me than I had anticipated. Being married and responsible for the well-being of my wife became especially difficult for me, after I was ordered to return to Britain.

The RAF wanted me to complete my contract with them in Manchester. Any romantic notions I might have had about a life lived large in an occupation zone were dashed by being posted home. My orders were irrevocable and absolute, and I had no other option but to obey them and return to England without my new bride.

My superiors assured me that in due course I would be permitted to arrange for Friede to follow me to my new post in Manchester. Although, in typical military fashion, they were not exactly sure how it was to be done, only that it would occur. "Your wife will be given a travel warrant, LAC Smith, when you are sorted in your new placement. Don't ask us how because this is the RAF and things have a way of working themselves out."

My transfer was devastating news to me. It ruined my dreams of remaining in Germany and keeping my new wife cocooned in the safety of her family and friends while I made plans for life outside of the Air Force. Reassignment left me worried and frightened by my new responsibility of trying to integrate my wife into the-*if there be muck, there's brass world* found in the north of England.

Being Friede's husband in Germany was a lark compared to what I knew awaited me in Britain. While stationed in Hamburg, I was part of the conquering forces, and any problems that arose for her or me were easily overcome because I was a well respected member of the RAF. In Hamburg, my uniform gave me an influence I never had in British civilian life. It allowed me to do something that was impossible for me to even dare to contemplate in England: determine, for the good, the fate of myself and those that I loved. In Germany, I was able to use my authority to keep Friede and her family alive during a terrible time known as the "Hunger Winter." It was pretty obvious to me that once I returned to Britain, my ability to manipulate events for the well-being of Friede or me was going to cease to exist.

The night before I flew out of Hamburg for London, my new circumstances began to eat at me like scabies. I was frightened at the prospect of trying to make something of myself in a land abundant in rain, shoddy housing, limited opportunities, and soot. My depressing former life looked like it was racing to catch up with me and clout me on the back of my head.

"It will be right as rain, luv, you'll see," I told her when she started to look upset at the notion of abandoning her friends and family for a life across the North Sea.

I might have convinced Friede, but an inner voice told me something different. It was what my grandmother has said once to me as a child: "Yer Barnsley bred and born, and nowt going change that." On the eve of my departure for Britain, it appeared that being from the north was more a curse than a blessing.

I didn't let on to Friede that I was petrified. I was horrified that if she knew what awaited us in England, she'd whisper *auf wiedersein* to me. I don't know if it was due to my omissions, my forced optimism, or her general love for me, but she assured me that night she had no regrets about our marriage or my transfer. "I will follow you even to the ends of the Earth, but first you must make all of the necessary arrangements."

Chapter Two:
The Midlands

In November 1947, I was repatriated to Britain from Germany on a military transport plane. The moment I touched down at Gatwick, I sensed that this was perhaps the cruellest month to return to the land of my birth. Everything around me was washed in a grey light that reflected down from a dull and discontented sky. When I entered the capital, the people looked dreadfully bland and unhappy. It looked like a city that was just holding on out of sheer stubbornness. There was little evidence to me that anything joyous had happened in the metropolis, since 1939. The residents of this once majestic city looked haggard while their eyes appeared to be empty of emotion. People shuffled about like the elderly on the verge of senility unsure, uncertain and afraid. It depressed me to see London and her people so beaten, so tired of life that they were ready to throw in the towel. The city looked as sad and sick as some of the cities I'd seen in Germany.

At my train station the people looked no better. They wore old battered clothing and their faces looked weary from trying to get on with their lives in a city still suffering from the after effects of the war. While I made my way to the railway platform I heard commuters complain that parts of the east end were still bombed out. "After all this time, you'd think they could get the dustmen to haul away the mess."

"On our street, we had men from the UXB squad come and detonate one of Hitler's presents that he sent us in forty-two. Bloody shameful, that is; war's been done and dusted for over two years now, and the Jerry's are still knocking us off."

"But you got to say that Princess Elizabeth's wedding was smashing."

"Wasn't it? Just like a bleeding fairy tale. She's such a beauty, and he's a handsome devil. If my Bert were only half the man the prince is."

As their conversation floated around me like a sheet of newsprint caught in a gust of wind, I was relieved that I had missed the jerry-rigged splendour of the princess royal's wedding. It had occurred a

9

week before I arrived but the propaganda machines were still pushing out saccharine dipped headlines about the glorious event. The newspapers out on display at the kiosks dripped adoration for the royals and spoke of their regal love for us, the common people. Apparently, we were blessed as nation to be ruled by those with better blood and better sense than us ordinary plebs.

Angrily, I lit a cigarette and wanted to shout out *why is it that the royals, the aristocrats, and the landed Tories always expected the lower orders to suffer the famine? Yet, when its time for the feast, we are never invited, except as humble spectators or servants. It was the same with the royal wedding. It was just another version of Roman bread and circuses.* As I dropped my cigarette onto the filthy railway station's floor, I knew that although the masses liked a good spectacle and the royal wedding might just have fit the bill. Yet, the event to me, seemed to be out of place, out of touch and gauche because despite the cant from the media, that newly wedded couple didn't represent the best of Britain, just the most fortunate.

Sod it, I thought, Send 'em to heaven in a corn beef tin and let them meet St. Peter for their judgement day. As for me I had more pressing matters to attend to than to worry about the royals, their marriages, their, profligacy, their abdications and their obsolescence.

After innumerable delays on the train line, I eventually arrived at my base RAF Ring Way very late in the day. It was a large cold, impersonal outpost that bustled with vehicles, the never ceasing sound of thousands of men marching without purpose in their issued boots and the roar of arriving and departing aircraft.

I presented my transfer papers to a sergeant-major who was clerk to the base's adjutant officer. The NCO looked me up and down as if I were a grinding gear in some foreign machine. At first, I thought he was going to ask a subordinate to "Git hammer out and bang on it till the bloody racket stops." Instead, he deferred to his lieutenant, who seemed bored by my very existence. Wearily, he informed me that everything was in order but that "We'll have none of that slackness you lot got up to in Germany."

I thought it best not to disagree with his assessment, no matter how wrong or idiotic it sounded. *No point making enemy's your first day*, I said to myself.

10

That evening I was assigned sleeping quarters in a Nissen hut. It was boiling over with boisterous teens that made it hard for me to fall asleep. All their talk, their youth, their lack of experience made me feel ancient and worn out. I knew that they had spent the war close to their mothers' apron strings. I wanted to weep into my pillow from exhaustion and from the pain at being separated from Friede.

When dawn finally arrived, I was frozen stiff because no one had lit the fire in the stoves at either end of the hut. An NCO came in and cried, "Wakey, wakey." By that summons, my new life at Ring Way officially began. While the rest of my hut mates began to stir from their dreams of football, beer, and girls, I quickly dressed and left the hut.

Outside, I walked towards a building where one could wash up with hot water. The sky above me was a tempest of black clouds, while the ground beneath me was covered in granules of dirty snow. I could see my breath, and my hands were red with cold. On the way, I started to smoke a cigarette, but it tasted harsh and cut into my chest like razor wire. I started to cough and spit out loads of phlegm from my tobacco exhausted lungs.

When I got to the building, there was a line of men waiting their turn to get in and have a shave. I smoked another cigarette and muttered under my breath about the wait. Once inside, I found an empty sink, where I wet my face and then applied some lather with a coarse soap brush. I started to shave the stubble covering my face. After I had cleaned myself up, I looked at my reflection in the mirror and wondered who that old codger glaring back at me was. I looked a mess; my hair was thinning, my skin was the colour of cigarette ash, and my eyes were small, exhausted, and lifeless. I looked beaten and forlorn, and it frightened me.

I wiped my face dry with a towel, and then lit another cigarette. I walked outside, where the wind lashed my exposed skin. I wanted the breeze to thrash me senseless and blow away my feelings of decrepitude. I didn't know how I was going to survive the rest of my term of service. More importantly I wasn't even sure what I was going to do for a profession after my time was done with the RAF. I started to panic and I thought I had buggered everything up for Friede and myself.

11

"You're done for, mate, truly done for," I whispered while the fag end singed the tip of my thumb. I flicked the cigarette to the ground and grew nauseous inside the pit of my stomach from self-loathing. I was a bloody fool, I thought, because I had fallen for my own lies. I had tricked myself into believing that being in love with Friede and gaining her love made me invincible, made me special and deserving of a better life.

It didn't mean anything of the sort; in fact, my attachment to Friede was probably causing her more harm than good. I was endangering her future because she trusted me to know what the right path was towards our personal fulfilment. The problem was, I didn't know. I didn't have a clue. On that day, if somebody had asked me which way was up or down, I would have shaken my head and said, "No idea, mate." I started to think that perhaps her willingness to follow me to Britain was a disaster waiting to engulf us both.

It was not only my marriage that had thrown me into funk but the mindlessness of my tasks at Ring Way. My superiors had me execute one senseless order after the next as if I were in a glasshouse and being punished for some unknown transgression in military law. They put me in charge of a squad of blotchy faced recruits and each day, apart from Sunday was filled with the same insane order.

"Have the lads fetch sledge hammers and then, march them to the cinderblock building up the road from the parade square. Inside you will find a room filled with surplus transmitters, radio receivers and radar paraphernalia. Smash it all to Kingdom come, and never you mind the whys and the wherefores, it is not your business. Just remember that the room will always be filled with shite that needs busting up for as long as you live."

The equipment that had been vital during the war and paid for by lend lease, war bonds, and death duties was now considered superfluous. Like so many other things of value, the armed forces and the government preferred to destroy it rather than let them fall into the hands of the public or enterprising individuals.

After several meaningless days of bashing and smashing radio receivers, I wrote in despair to my sister Mary. She was employed as a mill worker in one of Bradford's wool mills, and I asked her advice about finding work in the city. *The looms never stop,* she replied, *but are you up for it after living the life of Reilly in Germany? The pay is alright, but the noise is like the roar over the moors, when the wind goes to battle with the rain. It'll be a piece of cake for you to find some work, but what about your missus? The way you described her to me when we last spoke, she sounds right delicate. I am sure your lass is lovely and all, but work in mill is not for the faint of heart. Never you-mind, I am sure you'll make do and land on your feet. Didn't our Dad used to say to us, 'It'll be right as rain' or some such shite, like that, when money were tight and mum were caterwauling that it was all his fault that we didn't have a pot to piss in?*

In her letter, my sister also informed me that housing was scarce: *It is the kip that is the bother. There's nowt to let across the north. You'll be lucky to find a stone privy to call home. Everything has already been taken by the lads demobbed in '46. They were the ones who didn't muck about. They took their Army kit off straight away, got married and made bairns or vice versa. Besides, you wouldn't recognize Bradford or even Halifax. It looks like half of Europe dragged themselves to Yorkshire on a bus man's holiday. It is ripe with Poles, DPs. and Italian POWs. Mind you, the lasses really want a go with Italians because they are right good looking, like movie stars. But that doesn't fix your problem of a roof over your head and coal burning in the grate. I hate to say it because you are going to get brassed off, but the only one who can help you get sorted is our mum. But I guess that is sort of like asking the devil for a fiver because in the end it's going to cost you ten.*

I didn't find my sister's words very encouraging. The few friends I still had in Halifax were not any more positive when they answered my letters. They all agreed good housing was hard to find but that I should be optimistic. Easy for them, I thought, they had families that weren't balmy and the scorn of the neighbourhood like mine was.

There were few options left to me. I could to either write to Friede and say don't come, forget me, please go and live your life as if we had never met, or I had to reconcile with my unstable mother. It was a difficult choice to make because my mother and I had been estranged for years. We were at loggerheads for a hundred cuts each had done to the other's heart and soul during the Great Depression.

After I stared long and hard at the wallet sized photo portrait of Friede, I humbled myself and wrote a note to my mother. I asked her to put us up until I got back on my feet and could find something more suitable. Her response was quick and guarded: *For thee and thy wife, there be a room in the attic. I'll do it up right and proper for thee and put on a new a lick of paint for good measure. But remember you are not a wee lad anymore. I can't be running after you and wiping your runny nose. It's time that you stand on your own two feet. So it will cost you to come and live at home again, because your mam is skint as ever. So remember you should be looking after your mum now instead of it being ass over kettle. So, you are welcome in my house, even if you wed a German. But it'll cost you 10 shillings a week, plus your food. I hope that German girl of yours knows how to clean because we aren't like those filthy Europeans. We like things done proper.*

I sent her a curt reply and agreed to her terms. There was no other choice because I was anticipating that my demob from the RAF was fast approaching, and no one else had offered me a room to let. Along with the letter, I enclose five pounds as a Christmas gift to my mother. In the note I wrote, considering that I was expected to pay full board for her attic, that this was all I could or would spare her. I also told her that in spite of the fact that, years ago, she had travelled to London to have a naughty weekend with an Irish labourer didn't make her an expert regarding the hygiene standards of Europeans.

During that month of December and through the Christmas holidays, I became deeply depressed. I longed for my old life back in Germany. Everything around me seemed more dingy and backwards compared to Europe, including the food, the people, and the camaraderie. The longer I stayed at Ring Way, the more sullen and morose I became because I thought I had ended up in a cesspool. I also began to detest the peace time Air Force which had an overabundance of boot polish, boot licking, and perfectly creased trousers.

It didn't help my mood that I was not well liked on the base and my opinions were not tolerated by the younger recruits. For them, I was a museum piece from the last war. They called me the "the old man" and they couldn't understand why I still remained in the RAF. Once while I was in a line up for breakfast, someone said to me, "Oi, granddad, what you hanging 'round here for? Isn't it time you were off home to grandma?"

"Piss off, are you sure you can handle drinking that cup of tea, in your hand because you don't look like you're old enough to be off your mam's tit," I shouted back at him.

As for my superiors, they saw me as a malcontent because I was an individual who hated the rigidity and bureaucracy of the post-war

RAF. As I failed to say to my superiors "Yes sir, no sir, and three bags full, sir," I was considered a trouble maker by most of the NCO's who regularly told me to "Quit your griping, Smith, nobody asked you to sign up for a three-year stint. You'd done your bit in the war and should have buggered off home. Instead, you went and got wed to a bleeding Nazi."

I knew I had to get out of the services before I went mad. Fortunately, I was aware that there were two ways to wriggle out of my thirty-six month contract with the RAF: one, I could be killed while on active service; or I could follow a more sensible exit. My contract with the Royal Air Force allowed for either party to dissolve their obligation to the other if the agreement was rescinded within six months of its signing. There was no penalty, except I was obligated to return my £20 reenlistment bonus.

By January, the only impediment holding me back from leaving the services was that I needed to get my wife out of Germany, and I required the RAF's assistance to do it properly. Unfortunately, at Ring Way, the officers and NCO were rather obtuse to my desire to be reunited with Friede. "Tough bloody luck" was the average response by the NCOs to news that I was married to a German.

Anytime I complained about being separated from my wife, I received no sympathy. My personal happiness was not their concern. "The RAF is not interested in your personal life, L.A.C Smith. If you want to be reunited with your wife, fill out the proper forms and go through the correct channels."

"But there are none, sir. I don't even think there is a requisition form because I am the first man on this base to be married to a German," I pleaded.

"Right you are then," said the sergeant- major. "I guess you will have to wait until the RAF catches up with your modern thinking."

RAF Ring Way was never going to catch up with the twentieth century, let alone my predicament. It was a backward and unhappy place that could never have existed during the war. The camp was senselessly brutal to new recruits. The NCOs were Jesuits when it came to humiliation and torment. It was their objective to crush an enlisted man's spirit, and they did their task with blatant delight.

At Ring Way, I saw more toothbrushes employed to scrub floors than to clean teeth. Any infractions of the King's regulations, from improper saluting to marching without the proper heartiness, were considered a dereliction of duty. It appeared as if everyone in the low ranks was either being written up or on charges or being forced to march at double time to purify themselves of some crime committed against an NCO.

In Manchester, I was like an animal caught in a trap, and no matter which way I turned, the leg hold grew tighter. There seemed only one means to get my wife repatriated, and that was through sheer bloody-mindedness. Many times after tea, I tried to collar a sergeant- major to seek his help with my problem, but I was always brushed off with "Why did you go and marry a ruddy foreigner - and a bloody Jerry to boot?"

I grew so desperate; I followed one of my NCOs to the bog and tried to get his attention after he had done his business. I begged him to get the base commander to sign the travel order that allowed my wife to enter the country. He was having none of it. "You didn't need to go and marry a bit of what's your fancy across the waves. All you did was make your life miserable. And right now, all yer doing is getting me barking mad with your long face and your constant jibber jabber about your missus."

I was persistent, and I refused to give up, so finally, after much hectoring, Friede was permitted to leave the British occupied zone in Northern Germany. The RAF in Hamburg gave her a travel document, which allowed her a one-way transit to the U.K. Her date of departure was scheduled for the latter part of February.

"Mind you, Smith, don't get any ideas about living off base as you did in Hitler land," said my sergeant- major. "When your missus comes, you'll have to find her digs for herself and drop by for tea when I say so," he said with malice.

A little later on, the adjutant officer reluctantly agreed that Friede could be flown out of Germany on a military shuttle to London. When the news was given to me by my sergeant- major, I said, "I shall need leave and a travel warrant to bring her to Manchester."

"Sunshine, you'll be asking me next for a bloody staff car," he said with derision.

I shuffled uneasily on the balls of my feet and thought; *You are a proper toss pot.* I tempered the tone of my voice and replied in a mellow manner, "Sir, the quicker this is done, the faster you will have me out of your hair."

He thought about it for a while and said, "I will arrange it with the duty officer. He'll sort out your pass and travel warrant, but you'll get no more than twelve hours leave to do your dealings. So what do you got to say to me now, sunshine?"

"Sir?" I asked puzzled.

"Smith, you should kiss my bloody arse for showing you such a good turn. Mind you, I expect something in return, especially after you've brought your war booty bride back to the midlands." He made an obscene gesture with his fingers and cackled with a smoker's laugh.

Chapter Three:
The hours separate us

The week before Friede arrived, a cauldron of sub-arctic temperatures formed over the pack ice at the North Pole. If it were not for an ambitious jet stream, those Palaeolithic temperatures would have remained buried at the top of the Earth; instead, the intemperate air was grabbed in the talons of a leeward wind that swept towards Scandinavia and onwards to the rest of Europe.

Even the North Sea wasn't strong enough to stop the brittle cold from billowing across the waves and landing on the shores of Scotland with a frozen fury. The harsh atmosphere gathered its strength in the lowlands and grappled up the highlands until it reached Hadrian's Wall. From there, like a barbarian hoard from a Norse saga, it marched across the English border until it reached RAF Ring Way and turned everything around me into a frigid mess.

No one was prepared, after a relatively mild winter, for the ferocious wind or the numbing cold that tore through Yorkshire, ate up the Midlands, and ripped into the southern Home Counties. Across Britain, coal fires were lit in a million grates "to stop the bloody draft from breaking down the doors."

It was hard for anyone to keep warm in terraced house Britain, and people did what they had done for generations when the temperatures dipped. They stayed inside, wore double pullovers, and if possible, they kept well under their bed covers; otherwise, they congregated around glowing hearths in their parlours and complained about the cold and drank numerous cups of tea. If they were lucky and had some spare cash, they ingested liberal amounts of medicinal, brandy, gin, or whatever spirit was available. It was the favourite remedy for many of England's grandmothers, who swore that "it takes the chill from thy bones that bit of whisky before bed."

Every morning that our island was locked up in that deep freeze the dawn came reluctantly as a cat treading home on snowbound streets. For the common airman at RAF Ring Way, we faced the cold on the parade square with ill humour. Many an enlisted man muttered "Bugger you" under his breath when ordered to stand to attention in the inhospitable climate.

19

After sun down, our huts were as comfortable as Scott's base camp on the shores of Antarctica. Once, the mercury dropped so low that it petrified exposed water, burst water pipes, and glazed every window on the base with a thick sheen of ice. Guards who stood watch over Ring Way pounded their feet onto the frozen ground to keep warm and cursed their bad luck not to be stationed in Hong Kong.

By the time my birthday rolled around on the twenty-fifth, the weather had not improved. In fact, the burly sergeant that came to rouse us at half-six confirmed my suspicion that February was a bleak month to be born. He cried out, while pulling bedcovers off of half dazed airmen that "it was cold enough to freeze a monkey's balls off."

Nevertheless, he still ordered everyone to get cracking and said, "You bunch of useless bastards' better get a move on or else you'll feel my boot on your arse."

I groaned at the thought of getting out of bed because even under my rough wool RAF blankets, I was frozen from the tip of my nose to the soles of my feet.

I braved the icy floor, dressed and left the Nissan hut to shave. The water was tepid, the razor blade blunt, and I nicked myself several times. Afterwards, with congealed drops of blood on my face, I ate my breakfast alone in the canteen. I noted that the porridge was lumpy, but it was piping hot and had a taste reminiscent of sand mixed with coarse oatmeal. As a birthday breakfast, I concluded that I had enjoyed both better and worse meals.

Afterwards, I left the relative warmth of the canteen to collect my men. Despite the numbing temperatures, I felt upbeat and optimistic because while I marched my men to the bashing shed, the sun suddenly pushed itself free from a gang of rotund grey clouds that concealed it. For a moment, a bright and happy beam of light caressed my face with a warm and welcoming sensation. I dreamed it was a kiss blown from Friede's lips to me.

Those few rays of light buffeted my mood throughout my work day while I supervised the pulverization of RAF electronic equipment. After my shift, I left camp and took myself to a local pub. I thought it was appropriate that I celebrate my twenty-fifth year with a whiskey. I wasn't bothered that there was nobody in the pub that knew or cared that it was my birthday. The smoky dram was to be enough cheer for me that night. It warmed my soul while I happily spent my night re-reading a letter Friede had sent me for the event. Her words reassured me that she was still in love with me. *It is no longer months or days, but only hours that separate us now....*

Friede added in her note that she was excited by the prospect of coming to live in Britain; however, there was an undertone of concern in her letter, which hinted that she worried about my prospects in the civilian world. Yet, by the end of her missive, she returned to an unwarranted trust in my resourcefulness. *I am sure,* she wrote, *that you have it all planned out, so I will not fret about things I have no control over. Do you think there would be time, when I arrive, to visit London? I know that we must head back to your base in Manchester, but it would be lovely to see your beautiful capital.*

Her letter made me ecstatic, fearful, and tied my stomach up into knots at the mention of my plan. I had none, and as for sightseeing, that was out of the question because my travel warrant didn't allow for detours. For that matter, my wallet no longer accepted any extravagance because I was saving every penny I had for the uncertainty of demobilization. Knowing that her arrival to Britain was imminent, I understood that the die was cast. *Everything has got to work itself out one way or another, or else we are buggered,* I thought.

There was only one small favour I wanted now, but there was no one who had the power to grant me that request. I wanted the weather to make a turn for the better. I thought that the best way for Friede to be introduced to England was with a hint of spring in the air rather than the grit of winter. Sunshine, I thought, was going to be my best and only insurance against Friede being disappointed by the reality of post-war Britain.

Unfortunately, the cold weather refused to cooperate. It was steadfast and stubborn and wouldn't dissipate. Winter spread its icy, skeletal fingers across most of Europe. It fanned out from the Channel and moved down into the Hook of Holland, and then it pushed up towards Hamburg and Kiel. The cold front made life even more unpleasant for those in Germany who were still housed in refugee camps or were dependent on the Red Cross for their daily sustenance.

Hamburg encountered a paralysis in their food and fuel supply because of the frozen conditions. Yet, despite the inclement weather, the shortages and the brutality of daily life in the city, Friede and her mother, Maria Edelmann continued to make preparations for the trip abroad.

When it came to living on the edge of destruction, mother and daughter were seasoned veterans. Five years of war and the consequences of surrender had taught them to be shrewd in matters of everyday commerce. They both agreed that it was necessary that Friede have some warm clothing and undergarments for her new country. "The shops are probably full of clothing in England," Friede's mother told her, "but your man will appreciate a thrifty wife. In summer, you can ask him to buy you a whole new wardrobe, but for now, go prepared."

So the women scoured the black markets, looking for appropriate clothing. After much hectoring, bartering, and bickering, Friede chastised her mother. "Mutti, there is only so much I can pack and bring with me on the plane."

"Alright, child, but we must now buy some presents for your husband's family in England," responded Maria Edelmann.

Friede agreed that this was a very important matter. "I don't want them to think I come from rude or ungrateful people."

Friede's mother laughed and said, "Child, they already know that you come from a very good family. Harry's love for you should prove to them how special you are. He can't hide his affection for you from anyone, especially his family."

As they made their way home, Friede said to her mother, "This cold is incredible. I don't remember winter being this uncomfortable before the war."

"I don't know," replied her mother, "winters come and go. Sometimes they are mild, and sometimes bitter. It is like life: there are good days and bad. Let us just be thankful that we don't live in the Russian zone because there it must always feel like February, even when it is July."

"It is very frightening what those Reds are doing in the east," continued Friede's mother. "They are just as bad as the Nazis. It is all a bunch of rubbish when people say the Russians occupied East Germany to punish us for what we did to them on the Russian front.

They want an empire, just like Hitler did. Just take a look at how they destroyed Czechoslovakia's democracy, only days ago. Nobody can tell me that that is not the work of the devil.

"What happened?" Friede asked, puzzled.

Her mother turned to her with a look of disapproval and said, "Once in a while, you have to listen to news on the wireless rather than just Radio Luxembourg. The Soviets staged a coup d'état in Prague, and now the Czechs, like everyone else east of the Oder river, are a vassal to Stalin."

"Yes," Friede remarked, "it sounds terrible." Friede was reluctant to speak further about the sad politics of the day with her mother, but the ache to ask her something just as important was too great. "Do you think my father is still alive in Berlin?"

"I don't know, child. He left us when you were a baby and made his life without us in the capital. It would be hard to believe that he survived the final months of the war and the Red assault on Berlin. If he did, I don't know how he could have escaped the murder squads of drunken Russian soldiers who raped any german woman on the street and shot dead any man who protested their barbarity."

"It is prudent," her mother said reflectively, "to put your thoughts towards England because that is your future and Germany is your past. Britain is full of possibilities for you, if you put your nose to the grind stone."

Friede smiled and put her arm around her mother and said, "I think everything is going to be alright once I get to Britain. I will be able to send you lots of supplies and money because I am sure that England must be stuffed full of food and everything else you can imagine that makes life worth living."

Her mother nodded in agreement. She didn't say anything more because she didn't want to spoil their loving mood. Friede's mother knew it was for the best that her daughter leave Germany, but she was also old enough to know that life doesn't always work out as planned.

During Friede's last days in Germany, she was filled with moments of breathless excitement over the prospects of a new beginning. Friede was also touched by a sense of overwhelming melancholy that smeared her happiness. The realization that she was

23

leaving her childhood and youth behind was most evident when she said farewell to her closest girlfriends, Gerda and Ursula.

Friede burst into tears when they all met for a final meal at one of their favourite restaurants before she flew to London.

"Don't worry," both of her friends said because "before next Christmas, you will be back for a visit."

"Do you think," asked Friede with uncertainty.

"Sure," said Ursula. "And by then you will have loads of gossip to tell us, about how your new life is going in England."

"Just think, you are going to fly into London, the capital of Britain, and we are stuck in dull old Hamburg," said Gerda.

It took some time, but Friede's confidence was eventually bolstered by her friends' encouragement and recounting of their shared past. They sipped on cheap schnapps and toasted their comradeship. "Even if we had champagne," Friede remarked, "it would still not do justice to the strength of our friendship."

The three women had shared an endurable and deep love for each other that had fortified them during extraordinary times of danger and privation in Germany. Their friendship had outlasted childhood, Germany's depression, Hitler, the horrors of the war, and the pain of the reconstruction. It was a testament to each of their characters that they remained loyal to each other in an era of betrayal and falsehood.

As the evening began to wind down, Gerda and Ursula bid her be safe and careful in her adopted country. "Don't trip over your emotions," Gerda warned her. "Be like the duck, and let the water glide over your back."

In a moment of reflection, Ursula confessed, "You know, I was always dead set against your marriage to a foreigner, but I think it was just because I was jealous. I didn't want a Tommy to take you from us. To leave Germany is your destiny, and a bright future awaits you, even if it is far from us." Ursula wept softly and confessed, "I will always love you, wherever you live in the world."

"I don't know what I would have done without having you two when I was growing up," Friede said to both of them.

Afterwards, Friede promised her two friends that she would write them, not forget them, and cherish the times they'd spent together. "I will return to my beloved Hamburg, and also to you, my sweet friends, as soon as time permits."

Friede spent her last night in Germany, alone with her mother in their apartment. The two women sat close to each other on a chez lounge that was situated near a wood stove, in Friede's bedroom. The timber in the stove crackled and hissed while it burned in its cast iron belly. The mother and daughter noted that even with the stove blazing, the windows in the apartment had frosted over.

"I hope they have good stoves in England," Friede's mother said.

Friede said with the surety of the untraveled, "Of course, mutti. There will be no worries about comfort in Britain. They have all the coal in the world. I will be just fine, so don't you worry."

After mother and daughter had talked nostalgically about old times, Christmas, and people from their past, they grew silent. It was as if they had awoken to the enormity of what was to occur the next morning. As the night wore on, Friede grew agitated because her departure from Germany was imminent. She realized that she was embarking on the greatest gamble of her life. It distressed her to know that nothing was going to be the same again for her. Whether she liked it or not, she was a grown woman. She alone had chosen this path, which was about to separate her from those that she loved and the places where she felt the most comfortable.

That night, Friede hoped that she had made the right choice by marrying me and immigrating to Britain. It was a lot to digest, but she realized that she had renounced her old life for the sake of one man. It frightened her when she thought that in the morning she would leave everything that she loved passionately, her family, her friends, her city, and her culture. Friede was giving everything up for a man she didn't really know.

Her mother sensed her daughter's ambivalence. Maria Edelmann attempted to reassure her by telling her that should everything end in tears, there was no crime in returning home.

"Child, I know men and the world. I don't doubt your husband's love and adoration for you, but sometimes love does not outlast May. So, there is no shame if for whatever reason you feel that it's best to return to Hamburg. There will always be room for you under my roof and at my table. Whether you are near or far away, you are my only child, you are my daughter, and I will never stop loving you."

On the following morning, at Fuhlsbüttel airport, Friede boarded a plane with RAF markings. From the nearby road, Maria Edelmann watched the plane taxi out onto the runway and take off. She tilted her head upward and watched her daughter's aircraft fly off into the sky. Her mother kept her eyes fixed on the aircraft until it was a blemish on the horizon. When there was nothing more to see, Friede's mother walked home to her apartment, which was located ten minutes away from the airport.

At home, Maria Edelmann made herself a cup of camomile tea and sat down at the kitchen table. Her apartment was silent, and Maria Edelmann started to feel old and lonely. To reassure herself that she had done the right thing by encouraging her daughter to move to Britain, she reached into her purse and fumbled around until she fished out a photo.

The photograph was taken a long time ago, *a lifetime ago*, mused Maria. Still, it was one of her most cherished photos. It showed Friede as a new-born who from a bassinet stared up with vibrant and loving eyes towards her mother, who returned the infant's gaze with an ocean of love.

Maria Edelmann kissed the photo and said some words that she had often repeated to her daughter: "Be safe, be well, and please be happy." Maria Edelmann put the photo back into her purse and got up from the table. She knew that it was time for her to get on with her day because in Hamburg, life was measured in what you could trade on the black market, and sentimentality was now a pursuit for the very rich or the mentally deranged.

Chapter Four:
Reunion

Not the cinema, books, or the newsreels had prepared Friede for the experience of flight. From the moment the aircraft became airborne, she was exhilarated by the novelty and new sensation of being aloft. Friede also noted that there was something very sad about observing her beloved Hamburg through her porthole window because as the craft gained altitude, the city became smaller and more insignificant to her eye. Landmarks and people were no longer distinguishable, and everything below looked unreal.

Friede wondered to herself if that was why it was so easy for the American Air Force and the RAF to obliterate her city. Was it because from such a great height neither history nor humanity seemed real and everything looked inconsequential? Friede concluded that it must have at least been easier for the men on board the bombers to open their bomb bay doors and let five hundred pound explosives tumble to the ground and obliterate a civilian population. *When you're soaring through the stratosphere,* she thought, *you can't hear, from far below, the dying moans from those that are burning to death from phosphorous explosives.*

Within an hour of being airborne, the aircraft experienced turbulence, and Friede's wonderment turned to nausea because she was never one for choppy rides. Her biliousness became extreme when the plane skimmed through clouds like they were breakers on a rough sea. Friede's face changed to the colour of river clay as she fought back the urge to be sick. On a wooden bench opposite Friede sat a ginger haired guardsman who noticed her discomfort. He handed Friede a paper bag and through silent gestures made her understand its use.

As she retched, Friede hoped that the other passengers on the plane were not paying any attention to her. After she was finished, she didn't know what to do with the bag or its contents until the guardsman made a suggestion.

The soldier shouted over the prop engines, "I'd keep that bag handy, Miss, because we are a long way from terra firma."

Friede ignored his comments and took from her purse a peppermint. She placed it in her mouth and began to suck hard on it to take away the foul taste. She tried to avoid the guardsman's glances by turning her head towards the porthole, but this just made her stomach feel more uncomfortable.

This was something else that Friede found somewhat disconcerting; she was the only female passenger on board this RAF DC-3. The rest of the manifest was comprised of soldiers, air men, or military personnel being shunted on leave or on military business to London.

Being the only woman on board, the men naturally found her an attractive distraction in what was normally a dull flight. From all around the fuselage, eyes darted towards her to size up her beauty and see if they could divert her gaze up from the floor. At another time, Friede might have enjoyed being the centre of attention, but considering that she was tired, air sick and nervous about her future, the stares of everyone resting on her every action distressed her.

Her face grew flush when she caught a couple of the men leering at her legs, sheered in thin nylons. *Why can't they just stop behaving like boys,* she thought. Her irritation, however, was cut short because the need to vomit overcame her irritation at the gawking men. When she finished being sick, Friede looked up and saw that that the men's lust had evolved to amusement over her distress.

It was a relief for Friede when the aeroplane finally landed at Gatwick. She wanted to get away from her fellow passengers as soon as possible. Friede was mortified by the thought that these strangers were going to remember her as the German girl who couldn't stomach flying.

Apprehensively, Friede looked out of her porthole window as the DC-3 taxied across the tarmac to the terminal building. Before today, she had never been outside of Germany's borders. Friede sighed and thought her heart was about to break from the sadness of leaving everything and everyone she cared for back in Germany.

A gruff voice came from the cockpit and made her reminiscence vanish like smoke. It was the co-pilot, and he ordered an airman to unbolt the door at the rear of the aeroplane. When the hatch swung open, an icy wind crept into the aircraft. It smelled of diesel fumes and hydraulic fluid. The stench upset her stomach as much as the turbulence had done while they had been in the air.

The soldier who had given her the bag to be sick in noticed from across the aisle her uneasiness and reticence. "Chin up, lass, London's bark is worse than her bite," he said.

Friede smiled and said, "Thank you," but she could see from the desolate sky outside that London was in foul spirits. Involuntarily, Friede shivered like a cat treading near slushy water and did up the top button of her coat.

"Aye" said the solider, "bundle up tight, lass, because the city is brittle with cold and deep in snow." He noticed that stowed underneath Friede's wooden seat was a giant leather suitcase. It contained precious linens from her mother's house because her mother Maria had warned her before Friede left Hamburg, "The British may have won the war, but they have a lot to learn about comfort and good manners. Any civilized person must always have a set of their own linens, like one must have a change of underclothes."

"It looks like you packed half of Hamburg in that case of yours, lass. Da ya mind if I carry it for you?" Friede nodded appreciatively.

When everyone began to deplane, the red headed guardsman called back to Friede as she came to the exit, "Mind your head."

She ducked and looked outside and across to the airport terminal. Beside it, lorries and military personnel moved sluggishly about their business. Friede looked upwards and saw thick, ponderous clouds, which emitted a dull grey light. It was the same forlorn luminescence one would see in a doctor's surgery. She hesitated until a voice from behind called out and said, "No turning back now, Miss. Jump or be pushed, but you are over the drop zone."

Friede placed her patented leather high heeled shoes onto the metal ladder and began her decent onto English soil. Even though the steps had been wiped free of ice, it felt unsteady to her. Tentatively, she began her descent towards the ground.

As she walked across the tarmac, a damp bitter wind sawed through her nylon stockings. Friede looked around for me, but I wasn't there. Disappointed, she frowned and followed the other passengers through a doorway that led her to passport control. The guardsman lugged her suitcase and walked a few steps ahead of her to lead the way.

29

Inside, Friede was confused by the crush of English spoken around her. It was a cacophony of dialects, intonations, and emotions. To her ears, it was as jarring as cymbals clashing because she was only familiar with English when it was spoken in intimate circles in Hamburg. As she moved further down the terminal hallway, she kept wondering where I was at and thought in German, *Wo bist du?*

Friede was unsure of what she should do next. *Where is he? Am I early or late? What time did he say he would meet me, with bells on? Am I at the correct airport?*

As each minute slowly dripped away without any sign of me in the terminal, doubt and fear began to creep into her imagination. Friede craved a cigarette but was afraid people around her would think her a loose foreigner.

When the soldier carrying her suitcase noticed that Friede had stopped walking and now stood confused in the corridor, he called out to her "What are you doing, Miss? The exit is straight ahead."

"Moment," she said distractedly and with some annoyance. The soldier, she believed, was becoming too familiar in his tone towards her.

Stray thoughts, like street dust, clouded her affections for me, and she thought, *He better have a good explanation for leaving me all alone on my first trip to his country.* For the briefest second, she wondered if I had done a runner.

Hadn't one of her friends warned her of Tommy's bearing promises and gifts? "They will always disappoint you in the end," one of her girlfriends had told Friede after her wedding.

*

Disappointment was the last thing I had on my mind when I left Ring Way to rendezvous with Friede at Gatwick. My plans became unglued the moment I boarded my train at Manchester's Piccadilly station. Even in peace time, nothing ran to schedule. Britain was running like a broken clock, where time was arbitrary and at the whim of broken springs and unbalanced pulleys. Everything that had a timetable was at the mercy of every imaginable shortage from fuel to parts. On that day, my train was like a hundred other trains late or postponed because the coal allotment hadn't been delivered on time.

The rail lines were also cursed by uncooperative weather, which caused further delays to my journey. We moved at such a slow speed that I thought it was probably quicker for me to hop off and jog the distance to London. The ticket collector took note of my agitation and my sarcastic requests for an update on our estimated arrival.

"Keep yer knickers on. We are all in the same boat here."

"How much longer is this going to take?" I complained. "I am very late."

"Were all running out of time, mate, so wait yer turn."

I realized that it was senseless arguing with him. He was not going to understand that I had broken a promise to my wife. The day before she left Hamburg, I sent her a telegram. My static message pledged that I would *"see you at Gatwick with bells on, full stop."*

Instead, I was seated in a claustrophobic third class rail car brimming with travellers infected with colds, coughs, and long faces. With arms folded, I berated myself for my failure to retrieve Friede without making a bollocks of it. I was such a fool; I didn't even have any flowers for her because the mongers in Manchester only wanted to flog weeds dressed as posies. As for buying roses in the capital, I knew that if I lashed out on my RAF pay, we'd be living off beans for a week.

By the time my train reached London, I was haunted by a constant image of my wife waiting for me, alone and forlorn in her adopted land. Even if she forgave me for my tardiness, I knew I wouldn't have the mercy to pardon myself. I understood that this was just the beginning of her disappointments. It was bound to grow worse as we drew closer to the friendless severity of Lancashire and her new lodgings.

*

While my train trundled south on its way towards London, the ginger-haired guardsman kept Friede amused at Gatwick. As time wore on, he noticed Friede's face grow pensive and asked, "Are you alright, Miss?"

Friede didn't respond, and the guardsman drew closer. "Can I ask why you are here, Miss?"

"Here," Friede replied, puzzled.

"Yes, in London, Miss."

Irritated, she responded, "To meet my husband."

"Where is your man then?" he asked.

"He is on his way," she responded.

The recruit smiled and said with cheek, "Miss, a man would be a fool to keep someone like you waiting."

"He is in the RAF, but he's stationed up north," she said.

"Poor sod, he's way up there, and you're down here all alone," responded the guardsman.

"Something must have delayed him," Friede said with confidence.

"Sure, Miss," responded the guardsman as he ushered her into the passport control office.

Friede showed her identification and travel warrant to an RAF clerk, who looked at it with disinterest, whereupon he stamped it and handed the papers back to Friede. "Welcome to England, Mrs. Smith," he said, and then returned to his tasks.

At first, Friede found it strange that the official had referred to her as 'Mrs. Smith'. Her new last name sounded like it came from one of the English textbooks she'd studied as a teenager. Friede recalled how her instructor had forced her to repeat out loud the phrase "*Mrs. Smith is the wife of Mr. Smith. They live in London and drink tea.*" She giggled at the memory of learning English by rote with a language teacher that despised any other language but German.

Friede started to think that her new identity sounded liked an alias, especially if she compared it to her maiden name, Edelmann. Then she thought about what her mother had said to her in the days leading up to her departure. "You are lucky, very lucky that a good man wanted to share his life and his name with you. Your father never married me. I was just his sweetheart and you were just his bastard. What type of man does that to his child?"

By the time I got the airport, I was breathless, dishevelled, and embarrassed. I caught sight of Friede before she saw me and I wanted to burst out running towards her. I hesitated because after so many months apart, I was struck by her beauty and how out of place she seemed in the swirl of dull uniforms and overcoats that pressed passed her. Friede looked totally unique, and because she wore a verdant green coat, she looked to be in techno colour while everyone else around her was enslaved in a monochrome world.

Later on, I was to learn that the exquisite coat had originally been a heavy wool blanket. The seamstress, who had delicately sewn her silk wedding dress, had been commissioned by her mother to do an equally masterful job on the coat. "I want my daughter to look as beautiful as an English rose, but I want to make sure she is protected from their notorious chills," her mother had told the dress maker.

In her hand, Friede clutched a small brown leather suitcase. It was the one she had used as a child when she was sent to live with foster parents because her mother's lover couldn't abide children. Inside the overnight bag was enough clothing for a fortnight and two books: The New Testament and Goethe's poems.

Beside her stood the guardsman, who held onto the much heavier case with a familiarity that irritated me. When he saw me approach, he put down the case and I heard him say, "I'll guess I'll be going, Miss. Good luck with everything."

He walked away from me and started to whistle a tune. Slightly jealous, I wanted to say something sarcastic but instead cried out, "I am so glad I found you."

Friede didn't fly into my arms like a starlet from a Hollywood picture, but let me approach her. She looked relieved and irritated by me, and when we kissed, I thought her lips were less than eager for mine.

When I let go of her, she said to me, "I am so tired, so very tired. I would love to get some coffee and a piece of cake."

"Coffee? Love, you've got more chance of getting a magic carpet ride than real coffee in London," I replied. "Come," I said. "At the train station, we can get a biscuit and some tea before we head back to Manchester."

Chapter Five:
What ya having, luv?

A rusting commuter bus, which moved with the speed of an old horse on a predictable milk run, took us from Gatwick to the capital. The interior smelt of burning oil, petrol, and anonymous passengers. Halfway to the city, it began to rain, and hard black drops peppered the bus. Outside, everything looked desolate and far from civilization.

"It won't be long now," I said to Friede, who sat squashed beside me on a row of wooden seats at the rear of the vehicle. "In no time, we will be in London."

Friede nodded, distracted by the barren and derelict landscape she saw from her window. "It's different than I expected," she said dejectedly. Friede remained focused on the empty world outside of her window. Needing some reassurance for what she observed outside, she grabbed hold of my hand. "Will it be like this in Yorkshire?" she enquired.

"Sort of," I responded and squeezed her palm. "But where I come from, the land is untamed."

Changing the subject, she said, "It's funny, but I have never seen a picture of your mother's home. Is it like my Mutti's?"

It was a hard question for me to answer. I wanted to say that taking a snap of my mum's house would break the bloody camera lens. Instead, I said, "For a long while, love, my family have been simple workers. Like most everybody else in Britain, we live a terraced house existence."

"I don't understand," said Friede.

You'll see soon enough, I thought with dread. I then did what I should have done a long time ago and tried to explain to her the difference between the lives of common workers in Germany compared to Britain. "The conditions that an average bloke must tolerate in Britain are much more different than in your country."

"How so?" she asked.

"Well, for starters, the workers here have always got a raw deal from the land owners."

"I still don't understand," Friede said.

35

"Your country at the end of the last century realized that if it wanted to be prosperous, it had to make a social contract with their people. It was a pretty simple trade off: the lower and middle class were provided decent and affordable housing, slums were demolished, fair wage laws enacted, and pensions were created for those too old to work," I said.

"So what happened in Britain? Why was there no pact between the workers and those in power, like in Germany?" Friede asked.

"The monarchs, the landowners, the industrialists, and the church believed it wasn't necessary," I said. "They just thought everyone would keep buggering on and know their place, whether it was tilling a lord's field or working a mill owner's loom. The industrialists and the government, I believed, thought that poverty was just an unfortunate but necessary by-product of prosperity."

Friede looked confused and asked, "But why wasn't there a rebellion or revolution, like in Russia or in Germany?"

I laughed and said, "Because as a people, we like to complain. We like to grumble and whinge, but when it comes to rebellion, it goes against our ingrained sense of the natural order. I think most people believe this is just the way God designed things. We are a nation that ascribes to a world sharply divided between master and servant."

"But," Friede interrupted me, "every Brit I met in Germany, besides you and a few others, seemed to have a sense of superiority and arrogance."

"That is because they were conquerors in a foreign land. After the war, it must have felt like every day was Boxing Day for them."

"Why?" Friede asked.

"Because," I responded, "regardless of their low rank, there were a million defeated people below them who would bow and scrape and say 'Thank you very much'. However, once they returned home, all their sense of superiority disappeared, and I know they resumed their timid little lives. It has always been that way when we Brits go abroad and conquer foreign lands. We built an empire out of our own sense of personal inadequacy, greed, and mercantile Christianity. Off the island, everyone roars with bluster, but once we are returned to old Blighty, we take our caps off in deference to our betters."

Friede started to look nervous, so I decided to cease talking politics and jaundiced history. It was all beyond my control anyway. "Just ignore me," I said. "Things aren't that dark anymore. Besides, we have a government in power that says that it is working for all Britain's citizens, not just the rich."

"Do you think I will like living in your mother's home after you leave the RAF?" Friede asked me with a slight quiver in her voice.

I realized that I had said too much too soon, and I tried to calm her. "Don't worry. My mum's place will be fine, and it is only temporary. There are some really nice spots to live in Halifax, and I am sure we will be in one of them shortly."

She didn't look convinced, and I began to regret telling her so late in our relationship about the harshness of Britain.

Friede was silent for a while, then she asked, "But it will be alright for us because you have prospects, right? We won't be living like refugees?"

"No," I said, "never like refugees, but we need to stay at my mother's until we can get ourselves sorted."

As an afterthought, she asked, "Do you think your mother will like me?"

For the moment, I thought it best not to distress her further with any more harsh truths about my mother or Yorkshire. I told her, hoping that it was going to be the end of her questions, "My mum isn't like your mother; mine is rougher around the edges, and so is the neighbourhood she lives in."

A look of disappointment fell across Friede's face. I tried to lift her spirits by telling her that where we were to live had "some very nice parkland."

"Really?" she said, pleased.

"Yes," I said, then muttered under my breath, "but it is more like muck land."

Friede didn't look altogether satisfied by my lacklustre response but let it go. The window beside her was thick with condensation, and Friede began to spell out with her finger the word *Hamburg*. As quickly as she had written out the name of her city, she wiped away her handy work as if embarrassed.

"Tomorrow, everything will look lovely because it will be sunny," I said hesitantly. I wasn't really sure if daylight was going to make anything appear better to Friede. My frank talk about post-war conditions in Britain had disillusioned her.

It was too much information for her to absorb after such a long and difficult journey, and she said she was going to close her eyes and sleep.

When we entered London, she awoke with a fright and asked where we were. I told her we were in the capital and had to change buses to get to our train station. At the terminal, the bus driver opened the boot and pulled out Friede's luggage. We slowly walked up the rain-spattered street to a city bus that would take us to Paddington.

I carried her luggage onto the double decker bus that was going to take us to the station. Commuters behind us grumbled in accents thick with East End deviance. "Get a move on," someone bellowed behind us.

After we sat down, Friede pulled from her purse a compact mirror, flipped it open, and gave herself a disenchanted once over.

"You must be famished," I said.

"I just want get to the hotel and take a bath," she said.

"By tea time we will be there." I began to fret inwardly because I wasn't sure if the Bed and Breakfast had anything but a tin bath for their guests.

Friede began to point outside to the shop windows and said, "I would love to go in and see a real London dress shop. Just to look," she said innocently.

"Next time, luv," I said thankfully. "There will be plenty of time on another visit, but today we have a train to catch."

When we finally arrived at Paddington, Friede looked as if she were about to faint. Her face was the colour of chalk.

"I don't feel very well," she whispered to me. "Perhaps I am just hungry."

"There's a restaurant up ahead. We can get a bite to eat there," I said.

"The cafe will be fine," she said.

We walked through dirty glass doors into the railway tea room, which was clothed in a blue smoke from burning pipe tobacco and flaming cigarettes being exhaled from wan lips. The interior contained a couple of tables and chairs, for weary commuters. At the side of the front entrance, there was a counter to order sandwiches, sticky buns, or something to drink. Behind it there was a giant kettle, which sat on a gas hob in a state of constant boil. It was at the ready, waiting to serve the hundreds of commuters that rushed in for a cuppa before catching their train home or to work.

I put Friede's bags underneath a table, and we joined the queue. The matron behind the counter looked hurried, ill-tempered, and ready to smack anyone who made her job more difficult. She badgered the clients standing ahead of us. "Oi, get a move on, or your tea will be as cold as the Thames. Ouze about a biscuit, luv? It wuz baked fresh this morning."

By the time it was our turn, I called out for two cups of tea with milk and two spoons full of sugar. "Hold yer horses," she bellowed back. I turned to Friede and shrugged my shoulders as if to say, *This is London.*

"Right," said the matron. "What ya having to eat? Fancy a bit of meat and kidney pie?"

I saw the pies sitting on the counter, and they looked as if someone had turned them over with a spade.

"No," I said hesitantly. My answer seemed to upset the women.

"Come on, then, what ya having? I don't got all day."

Now, I really wasn't sure what to order for our lunch. Asking for a sandwich from the tea matron seemed to be begging for trouble, but Friede looked about ready to collapse. Suddenly, I noticed on the top of the counter, resting underneath a glass container, several pieces of cake.

They didn't look good or even appealing. The confection resembled what every train station in London and across the country had sold since Hitler had invaded Poland. It was something only appetising to a nation whose sweet tooth had been numbed by rationing and the scarcity of choice. The cake's icing looked like industrial paint, and the jam inside like a ruptured intestine.

Unfortunately, Friede was not used to bad service or shoddy looking food, but I was. I forgot that although my wife and her country had suffered much privation at the end of the war, they still had expectations when it came to food and its presentation. To them, it should at least appear edible, even if it failed to taste good.

Absentmindedly, I ordered the cake, and I heard Friede gasp in revulsion over my decision.

"What is it?" I asked.

Friede pointed to the cakes entrapped behind the glass covering. I now saw what upset her. On top of the pastry were several blue bottle flies that were making a nice meal out of our lunch. The flies walked across the cakes like a man strolls around his back garden grass with pride of ownership. When the clerk freed the cake from underneath its glass cover, the flies came along for the ride and sat at the edge of the plate, waxing their appendages. Friede's face grew white with disgust. She asked me in a tone loud enough for the woman behind the counter to hear. "Are the flies included in the price of the cake?"

The matron looked confused, then noticing that the queue behind us had grown longer, she hollered, "So are ya aving it or not?"

Chapter Six:
South to the Middle

While we were on the train to Manchester, we hardly spoke because London had left us speechless and defeated. We sat arms folded and stared out into the blank faces of strangers. For some time, we listened to the locomotive as it bumped and clacked against steel rails and moved us towards the Midlands. I opened a packet of mints and offered one to Friede.

Thank you, she mimed and traded me the sweet for an anaemic smile.

As we moved further from the capital, we trundled passed giant factories, foundries, and mills. They loomed from the rain-streaked window and startled me like a nightmare that grew in horror, and then subsided and disappeared into the shriek from the engine's whistle. The carriage was plunged into darkness as we ran through a long tunnel that had been cut through a hill over a hundred years ago.

When we emerged, the urban wastes were replaced by a forlorn rural landscape that was being beaten senseless by sleet, which poured down from black leaden clouds. We kept silent and let the rain and the wind outside do our talking. They had more strength than either of us, who were knackered in both body and mind.

"I am going to get some shut eye," I said to Friede, but she didn't answer me back.

She had already retreated into the emotionally neutral world of sleep. Friede's body was slumped over towards the window, which had cool moisture running down it. Her hands were folded tightly on her lap as if in prayer.

Good, I thought, *it is the best place for us because in the unconscious world, we're able to escape each other's company.* I dozed like a soldier on midnight guard duty, head in chin, eyelids fluttering for the slightest hint of danger.

When I awoke, Friede was still in a deep sleep. Even the screech from the train's wheels or the conductor barging through our compartment didn't startle her from slumber. I looked around our section with puffy eyes and a dry mouth. The upholstery on our seats was frayed, worn, and stained. The lights above us were sheathed in grime, which made everything else look duller, cheaper, and totally filthy.

Jarringly, the other passengers who sat near us came into my focus, and they looked as tarnished as the carriage. I thought how austere and rough everyone seemed on this train. It was as if hope had been knocked out of their hands by a bunch of thugs in a back street. *This is what eight years of rationing can do to a people*, I thought. *We are no better off than a bunch of beggars.*

Friede moved as if to wake but thought better of it and turned her head closer into the crook of her arm. I got up from my seat and went to the back of the train for a cigarette. I smoked my fag with other glassy-eyed passengers. They all looked worried and tired as they silently contemplated their own hard fought lives.

We certainly didn't look like the victors in a world war. In fact, we looked the opposite; we looked beaten and ready to throw in the towel. I extinguished my cigarette and wondered how Friede was going to make out in Britain - or for that matter, how I was going to.

From what she had experienced so far, I didn't think she had much hope of ever getting acclimatized. She was a stranger in a strange land, married to me a man with few prospects. I started to feel petrified about how our marriage would survive the North of England. How did anyone, for that matter, survive this country if you weren't born with the right accent and proper connections? It was only guile and cunning that had kept me and my family going during the Depression. As for living out the war, I knew I was a lucky bugger, but I wasn't sure if that would suffice for life after Hitler.

By the time we reached Manchester's Piccadilly station, it was half-past four. The terminal teemed with workers scattering towards home with sour expressions. I carried Friede's heavy case through the station to the street level. She walked beside me and held her small overnight bag in her hand.

"Everyone looks as sad as they did at Dammtor station in Hamburg during the ice winter," she remarked.

"Wait until Friday," I said. "Once they have a couple of pounds in their wallet and can go down to the pub for a pint, they'll spark up like a Christmas tree. I don't think anyone ever looks completely happy in this country unless it is the weekend or their summer holiday."

42

We walked away from the goliath terminal and out into a city that was rank with fumes from factories, lorries, and over-ripe rubbish bins that were drowned in the rain.

When we were on the bus to Ring Way, Friede asked me, just as a clippie was about to take our money, "How long will I be staying at this hotel?"

"It's not really a hotel," I replied, "but something more akin to a pension in Germany. I don't expect you to be there for very long, maybe a week at most. Once I tell my superiors I am breaking my RAF contract, I think they will put me off the base like the cat. Mind you, I have to pay them back the bonus they gave me in Germany for re-enlisting." It's a pity that they want it back. We could have really used that twenty quid as a nest egg."

"I am sure we will make do," Friede responded. "You always found a solution to our problems in Germany."

"Yes," I said without much conviction. I looked away from Friede and downwards to the aisle way. In my silence, Friede nervously played with her gloves, which sat folded on her lap.

It took around twenty minutes for the bus to reach our stop, which was a large village near my base, on the outskirts of Manchester. For a second or two, we stood at the side of the roadway and watched the bus disappear up the road into the dusky light of tea time. Except for a few cats vanishing into a narrow laneway, the hamlet was deserted.

"Come," I said and gathered up Friede's case and began to walk with a quicker pace because I was aware that my travel warrant was near expiration.

"We are not far from your home now," I said with lifeboat cheer.

Friede said with similar enthusiasm, "It looks like a very nice neighbourhood." When she had finished her sentence, her shoe sunk into a puddle of rain water that had gathered on the cobble stones. "Damn," she said with irritation.

"Don't worry," I said, "we are nearly there, just another minute or so."

The neighbourhood was populated by single and semi-detached dwellings. They had been built during the age of Victoria. This was once an area for men who wore starched collars on weekdays and stern faces at the local Anglican Church on Sundays. Each one of the homes was guarded by a low stone fence, and entry was granted through a creaky wrought iron gate. Most of the homes were dark and shut tight for the night. It was a neighbourhood on the precipice of middle class respectability that had started to tip into gentile poverty.

Friede asked me, "Does your mother's neighbourhood look like this?" I pretended not to hear and was thankful when we came to the front entrance of the boarding house.

"Here we are," I said cheerfully. "Perhaps not the Taj Mahal, but it will do for the moment."

Friede remarked with some uncertainty, "It's very quiet, and there is no name plate. In Germany, a pension must have a sign on its front entrance."

I nodded and said, "It will be fine inside. Brits just do business different than Germans."

"OK," she replied with resignation.

While we stood at the door, I made a silent prayer that this lodging house would make her transition to Halifax a little easier.

"How did you find this place?" Friede asked.

I explained that the landlady had been recommended by a fellow airman whose wife came to visit him on weekends. The owner, Mrs Chapman, had been taking in boarders since her husband died fifteen years previous.

I rang the bell, and after some shuffling behind the door, Mrs. Chapman slowly appeared. "Mr. Smith," she said. "I was expecting you and your wife much sooner than this hour."

She ushered us into the vestibule and said, "Come in quickly; don't want to let the heat run out and down the street." With a small degree of charm, Chapman introduced herself to Friede and asked about her journey. "It's a pity there was no sun today for you, luv, but that is England in winter. Come, I will show you to your room."

On the way, Mrs Chapman spoke to Friede and said, "Don't worry, luv, I'll take good care of you and make sure you are fed proper. I only accept in my house respectable girls who need a touch of home."

"Thank you. That is very kind," Friede said, and Mrs. Chapman spotted her German accent.

"You're a German, aren't you?" she said as if she had discovered a rare tribe of head hunters in the Amazon.

"Yes," Friede said cautiously.

"Never you mind, luv. I don't harbour any grudges over the war. Like I told your man when he let the room for you, I don't discriminate here. As long as they are good girls, I don't care if they are Irish, Scottish, or even German. I only take exception to the Poles. They're a dirty lot, even if they were our allies."

"Are there any other lodgers?" I asked.

"No. There are no other guests this week but your Mrs. Smith. So, I will give you all the special attention a new visitor to England needs."

Friede's room was on the second floor, and Mrs. Chapman opened it with an old key that rested on a chain that had perhaps fifteen similar keys.

The interior felt as cold to me as an airplane fuselage at twenty thousand feet above the North Sea. The room was very small but tidy and consisted of a bed, arm chair, and writing desk with a wash basin on top.

Friede looked at me and said she was cold. The landlady chirped in, "What, what?"

I rubbed my hands together and said it was as cold as being on the shores of Hudson Bay.

The landlady looked at me suspiciously and replied, "If I didn't mention it before, I will now. You have to pay for the gas heat separately."

She pointed towards the fireplace situated on the outside wall that was covered by heavy wall paper. Inside the hearth was a metal box attached to a gas pipe.

I looked at it suspiciously, and the landlady defensively said, "That is one of the most modern new devices for home heating. It costs a shilling for each go around with the heat."

"How efficient," I remarked cynically.

Mrs Chapman replied, "It makes each guest responsible for their use of coal. It's still rationed, you know," she said with some irritation.

At the side of the heater was a meter with a slot to feed your coins, like in a telephone box.

I fished around my pockets and found a handful of coins; I hoped it would keep Friede warm until I returned the following evening.

"I am afraid it only takes shillings; no tuppence or hay pennies," said Mrs Chapman. She was about to leave the room but stopped as if she had something to get off her chest. "I don't usually allow men to stay in the rooms of my female guests without a chaperone, but seeing that you are married..."

It was about to say something sarcastic when she interrupted me and said, "Included in the rent, your missus can have a good breakfast here and a cold plate for supper. If she wants lunch, she'll have to go into the village."

Mrs. Chapman made her excuses and departed the room.

I smiled at Friede and was about to give her a kiss when there was a knock at the door. Mrs. Chapman returned to say that she would come back in ten minutes with a cold plate and some tea. "Every one of my guests has told me I should win an award for my pork pie. After tonight, though," she said curtly, "you will have to take your meals in the dining room at the appointed time, which is five o'clock sharp."

After the landlady closed the door, I tried to kiss Friede on the lips, but she offered me her cheek instead.

Disappointed, I asked, "Is everything fine?"

She shook her head weakly in assent and responded, "It has been a long day, and I have to learn how to breathe in England. I'll be alright, just let me rest. It is marvellous what you have done. Now you should go back to your base, and I will get ready for Mrs. Chapman's world famous pork pie. I am sure diners in Paris would weep if they could get their mitts on one of her cold meat dinners rather than in one of those stuffy cafes on the Seine."

Chapter Seven:
Cashiered to Halifax

On my trek back to Ring Way, the black tide of night rushed in like a swollen river and drowned the last shards of dusk. I was exhausted, and it hurt to walk or to think about anything but sleep. The long journey to London and my return to Manchester with Friede had taken all my strength, and I had nothing left in reserve. All I wanted to do was get back to camp and shut my eyes. Along the way, I wished that someone would pass by and offer me a lift, but the road was quiet. Now and then, a few stray Lorries crept up behind me, blasted their horns, and disappeared into the diminished horizon.

When I finally reached base, the sentry on guard duty let me pass without a word. He didn't even bother to look at my almost expired travel warrant. Doggedly, I walked back to my sleeping quarters, puffing feverishly on a cigarette. Groups of young recruits stood in my way. They were huddled in great coats and ignored my determined footsteps around them. From the direction of the airport's runway, I heard the groan of an aircraft's Rolls Royce engines. I looked up and saw a plane lift into the murky sky and disappear.

The next morning, I awoke and realized that I had slept in my uniform. My hut mates thought I was out on the piss and ribbed me without mercy.

I ignored their teasing because I was confident that I'd be gone from Ring Way by the end of the week. My optimistic fire was quickly extinguished after I popped in to see the adjutant officer clerk following breakfast.

I wanted to set up a meeting with our commanding officer about my demob, but his clerk set me straight when he pointed to his superior's schedule book. There were so many dates booked with meetings. I asked the clerk sarcastically, "Are you trying to tell me that the adjutant is engaged for the next decade?"

"What good do you think is going to come your way by talking to me like that, sunshine? I can make your wait to see the adjutant seem a lot longer than ten years," rebutted the clerk.

We argued for several more minutes, but then the clerk suddenly grew tired of my persistence. "Alright, alright, I'll see what I can find for you. You are a pushy beggar. How does nine days from today sound?"

"It will do just fine," I said.

That evening, Friede asked me with a concerned tone in her voice, "Do you think the RAF will make problems for you?"

I shrugged and said, "I don't think so. I have done everything by the book, and there are no marks against my name. I can't see why they won't allow me to break my contract with them and leave the RAF, early."

Just as I was about to depart, I handed her some more shillings for the gas heater. Friede thanked me and said, "That blasted thing," and pointed to the meter, "takes your money like a bandit."

"Does it keep you warm?" I asked.

She laughed and said, "It does keep you warm if you throw some blankets on top of your body. Don't worry," Friede said and touched my arm. "I'll be warm enough when we can live together again."

I kissed her on the lips, but she broke away from me quickly, as if I were a stranger. "I am sorry," she said. "Everything is so strange for me right now. I don't feel like myself in this strange house."

"It must be hard for you," I said, "all of this change, and it has got to be a bit lonely, too."

"Thanks," she said, "But I am a lucky girl."

"Why do you say that?" I asked because at the moment I thought both of our fortunes were not at their best.

Friede's eyes glowed, and she said, "You always try to take care of me, so I should learn to be more patient and not complain. There are many others who have it far worse than me in Germany."

"Don't be silly," I said. "You are not complaining. It is a tough go trying to live in a foreign country, and getting used to its customs and languages. Besides," I said with some guilt, "the sun seems to be going down all over Britain while the rest of the world is getting back on their feet. Things will start to look up for us but we just have to give it some time," I said, trying to gather up my own self-confidence.

"I will," she said, but Friede still looked discouraged and said, "I wish you didn't have to go so soon. It is so dismal and lonely here with no one to speak to except Mrs. Chapman."

"I'll do my best to get this sorted soon," I remarked and left to return to Ring Way.

By the next morning, Friede was determined to keep her melancholy on a lead. Depression was not going to drag her into a reclusive life, locked up in a room on the edge of Ring Way. When Mrs. Chapman began to gather Friede's breakfast dishes, she asked her sympathetically, "What are you going to do today?"

"I will go out and explore your village," Friede said with a smile fixed on her face for a stranger.

"You're quite the independent lass," Mrs. Chapman chirped.

Friede was just about to walk out the door when the landlady asked, "Are you sure you will be warm in that coat of yours?"

"Very," said Friede, knowing that the green wool blanket coat was as temperate as fur and soft as silk. At the moment she reached the squeaking gate at the edge of the walkway, Friede breathed a sigh of relief because she felt free of watchful eyes. There really wasn't much to see in this provincial hamlet: a butcher shop, a tea and cake shop, the chemist, a post office. There was also a decrepit dress shop that employed a nosey old sales woman. Once, Friede went in to browse but left in a hurry after the sales woman began to question her nationality as if it were a matter for the police.

Friede also discovered a book shop. She spent many spare hours meandering through the book shelves, reading the titles and touching the spines of the books. She even asked if they had any books by Thomas Mann.

"Don't get much call for German writers," said the owner. "But we have some very good works by Agatha Christie." Friede concurred that the woman was a superb mystery writer.

When she was not walking, window shopping, or reading excerpts from the selected works of Goethe back in her room, Friede wrote letters to her mother and to her friends back in Germany. She struck an upbeat and cavalier tone in the letters to her girlfriends. Friede exaggerated the comforts of her accommodation and the quaintness of the village. She couldn't resist at the end of her missives to point out the absurdities of British manners, dress, and food. In

49

the letters to her mother, she wrote in an altogether different voice. She was more circumspect and alluded to her loneliness and uncertainty.

In the evenings, Friede was happily entertained by my company. She wanted me to divert her from any gloomy feelings that she accumulated during the day. "Tell me a funny story," she would ask.

I gladly complied and would recount something funny and harmless that had happened to me in the Air Force. Many times, she liked to gossip with me about long ago days in Germany, and on other occasions we played two handed whist while I sang popular songs. Each evening, when my time with her was nearly over and I was preparing to return to base, Friede asked, "When can we leave and start our new life?"

I didn't know the answer, so I always responded with the same line. "Soon," I'd say, "a matter of days. It can't be long; any minute now."

On the morning of my appointment with the adjutant, the sky above the Midlands stubbornly remained the colour of flint rock. It hovered low over the parade ground, ready to open up and weep a cold rain at the slightest provocation. The outdoor temperature wasn't yet confident enough to be warm, but I felt the approach of spring. A breeze blowing in from the south was more kind than harsh on my face and gloveless hands. It was now the second week of March; winter was nearly done, and I hoped that a new season dawned for me.

A clerk ushered me into my meeting with the Adjutant officer. The sergeant who had found my requests for Friede's repatriation troublesome was also present at this meeting. My commanding officer sat behind a fastidiously arranged desk. Its surface was clean of any clutter except for two telephones and a small photo of the officer's family that rested in a silver frame at the edge of the desk. On his neat desk, there was also a thin folder that contained my service record, a list of my postings, my training in wireless operation, and my performance ratings with the RAF since my induction in1941.

I saluted both of them, and they returned my salutation with less enthusiasm. I was instructed to be seated. The NCO remained standing while the commanding officer started to make notes on a sheaf of paper. For a second, I thought they had forgotten that I was present or that I even existed.

I focused my attention on a large portrait of the kind which hung on the wall behind the adjutant officer's desk. George V looked stern but fatherly and I thought, *well, your Highness, you better not have any complaints about me because I think I've done enough for you and your family.* My imaginary dialogue with our monarch vanished as soon as the adjutant officer cleared his throat and said, "The sergeant tells me you want out of the RAF?"

Looking at both of them, I knew it was sink or swim time.

"Yes, that is correct, sir."

At this point, the NCO interrupted the interview and asked his superior if he could question me. The officer nodded, and the sergeant spoke to me in a hostile and condescending tone.

"Didn't you, in September of last year, sign on with the RAF for three more years of service?"

I concurred.

"Then why do you want out of the RAF? Was it something we said?"

I responded politely to his questions and said, "It was a mistake to take the extra duty. I now realise that I am too old for the rigors of service required by the RAF."

"Too old, Smith?" barked the sergeant. "I have pimples on my arse older than you."

"I think," said the officer, interrupting his sergeant, "we are getting away from the point. You, L.A.C Smith, are legally obligated to fulfil your service with the King."

"Unless you get killed," responded the sergeant.

I paused and thought, b*ugger the sergeant; he has my number, but he doesn't get to choose my fate today.* I explained to the adjutant officer that "it states quite specifically in the regulations that within the first six months of the agreement that either party can opt out the remainder of the contract with no penalty, except repayment of the bonus awarded to me"

"So you have not spent the money awarded to you on beer and dolly girls?" asked the sergeant.

"No, sir, I have not touched the money. The twenty pounds is right here in my pocket. It is ready to be returned as stipulated to dissolve the contract." I reached into my pocket, but the officer shook his head.

"Not now, Smith. Let me see the extension of service papers that you are holding in your hands," the adjutant officer said sternly.

As the lieutenant read over my copy of the contract, he remarked. "You are cutting it a bit thin, aren't you, Smith? After all, your timing is a very close shave because your six month grace period is almost up."

I made some half-hearted apology but wasn't going to tell them the real reason for the delay was the wait for Friede's repatriation.

He handed me back the paper and said, resolved, "Well, we won't keep you if you don't want to be kept. Your record," he said, touching the file on his desk, "rates you as a superior Air Crew man. There are no stains in your copy book, so I am not going to put up a fuss."

"Thank you," I responded with a grin.

The officer added, "I'd hold off on that grin because I think you shall remember us fondly once you get back onto Civvy Street."

"Perhaps. But might I ask when that will happen?"

"We should be able to clear you out of here on the day of your six month anniversary, March sixteenth."

The sergeant coughed and said, "That is two days away, sir."

The officer looked at the NCO, then to me. "Is there a problem in sorting this out in forty-eight hours? Is L.A.C Smith doing anything especially important for the nation while in your care, sergeant?"

"No, nothing important, sir," said the sergeant.

"Well then, let's get this done and on the double. We don't want to waste a farthing with excess personal."

The officer looked at me and continued. "This new government; the one that your lot voted in," he said with a sneer.

"You mean Prime Minister Attlee?" I asked.

"Yes. The Labour government is hell bent in bankrupting and destroying the Royal Air Force, the Royal Navy, and the Army. So fly the coop, L.A.C Smith, and good luck to you because you shall need it in this New Britain your people created."

At this point, a gloomy silence similar to when a coffin is lowered into a freshly dug grave wafted through the room. The sergeant cleared his throat to gain the adjutant's attention.

The officer, with a hint of irritation, dismissed me. "Now as you can see, I have other matters to attend to, so from now on the sergeant will see to your discharge." I saluted the adjutant and disappeared from his office as quickly as I had entered it.

I left his office and made my way back to the parade square to collect my squad and bash electronic equipment to dust for one final day. As I marched my men to their work assignment, I thought, *it is all over now*. I was elated, but I was also despondent. So much had happened to the world, to Britain, and to me since I enlisted in the RAF in 1941. I had grown up and matured in both body and mind while civilization clashed on battlefields strewn across the world.

It occurred to me that since my induction in the RAF, I had saluted hundreds of NCOs and officers, from sunrise to sunset. I had saluted sergeants during squad bashing, at the end of forced marches, and after live ammunition training exercises. I had saluted officers while on parade or after a tongue lashing for misbehaviour. After seven years of service to the king, I had saluted my superiors across the British Isles and through Belgium and Holland, and finally into occupied Germany.

In my military career, I had brought my right hand to the brim of my cap and down to the side of my trousers over ten thousand times. Most of those salutes, I thought, were made with a flourish but with little belief or conviction. They were much like the motions I employed during communion as a small boy. The sign of the cross or the salute were done as a ritual to demonstrate obedience to an unseen cruel god or government and evade the wrath of priests or sergeants.

However, in my opinion, unlike the church, the RAF had been an honourable tribe. I was proud to have been a respected member and done my duty. In many ways, I felt better prepared for this uncertain peace because of my apprenticeship with the RAF. I entered the Air Force callow and naïve, but I left with a destiny to finally pursue. It wasn't a great, ambitious fate or reckless dream of fame and wealth that I claimed. I just wanted what had been denied my kith and kin in Yorkshire for generations. I wanted a chance for love, financial stability, and purpose beyond hewing coal from a seam deep below the Earth's crust. I realised that the RAF had turned me into a combatant. I was now prepared to fight and defend my dignity and my family's rights in the civilian world.

On my final day, it didn't take me long to pack up my belongings. I was asked to report to the paymaster to receive any money owed to me by the R A.F. I was handed a couple pounds and coppers and placed them in my wallet. My finances sorted, I was then ordered to the supply hut to begin my transformation into a civilian again.

In the cold supply hut, a clerk ordered me to strip down to my underpants. I stood shivering while a pimply lad noted in a ledger each item of returned clothing. The clerk then sized me up and said, "You look about the normal fit, so you can have your choice of suit. We have either brown or brown."

I said, "I guess I'll take the brown one then."

He handed me a thin single breasted suit, which felt like it had been woven with horse hair.

The clerk signed a piece of paper that said all that had been loaned to me by the state had been returned in good order. I was dispatched from there to the adjutant's office. A sergeant who I was not familiar with took my papers to the officer on duty. My papers were signed, and I was discharged from the RAF. Everything was done with as much emotion as if they were shipping a lorry full of beans back to the factory rather than discharging a human being from their service.

Contemptuously, the sergeant gave me a once over while I stood cocksure in my brown suit, which hung loosely on my shoulders. This sergeant gave me my final order, which was, "Well, that's sorted. Off you go."

My last day at Ring Way was very much like my first day in the RAF at Padgate: I was alone with only strangers for company. I had one last cigarette inside the compound at Ring Way. As I walked to the entrance, the sun was breaking out from the clouds. At the camp gates, I showed my discharge papers and felt cold in my new kit. The guard smiled at me as he would to a lorry driver delivering milk. "Terra," he said and handed me back my papers.

I walked out of the enclosure with long, proud strides. Way back in the distance, I thought I heard the bark of a sergeant on the parade ground. Maybe it was just my imagination, but I could have sworn that the NCOs ordered his squad for "eyes right." While I made my way down the road, the bellows from all the sergeants who had ever ordered me about followed me on the wind. The further away I walked from the camp, the fainter the voices grew, until all I heard was the sound of my own breathing.

The road before me was deserted, but I was not disappointed because I was on my way to gather Friede. My eyes were fixed, my orders clear; I was on the right path, even if it meant returning to my past, my mother, and her terraced house in Halifax.

Chapter Eight:
The Prodigal Returns to the rough and ready North

After my discharge, we left Manchester on the same day and travelled north on a regional bus to Halifax. There was no straight road to get to the Calder Valley; so our journey took us through Huddersfield, Elland, and a dozen other towns that had existed since the days of Viking subjugation. Along the way, the bus meandered from village to village and stopped to pick up new riders. The passengers were always rook-backed ancient relics, born long ago and now on the kerb side of life.

During our trip, Friede was all eyes and ears. She registered each new sound and sight as a unique experience. When an old man grinned and exposed more blackened gums than teeth at her, she smiled back at him as if she were being introduced to a relative. Across from our seat sat another man who rolled a cigarette with rheumatic hands that looked as course as grinding stone. She nudged me with her elbow and whispered, "I always wanted to learn how to roll cigarettes."

"Why would you want to do that?" I asked.

"All the liberated, intellectual women in Hamburg and Berlin rolled their own cigarettes." She laughed and said, "When I told my mother I wanted to roll my own cigarettes, she said she'd roll me out of the house if I even dared to smoke. Who are all these people on the bus?" Friede asked. "They are antique, and everyone looks like they have had a difficult life."

"Just locals," I responded with little enthusiasm. "They are probably out for a day's visit to see a relative or they are off to a market." To me, they were about as interesting as old worn rocks heaped up by the side of the road. I had encountered their type since I was boy in Barnsley and wanted to keep well out of their geriatric ways. The men had earned their living in the coal pits, and like my grandfather, my father, and my uncles, they were old before their time.

When she saw my jaw clench after I had looked around the bus, Friede asked, "What's the matter?"

"These old folks should be on the Saturday morning flicks," I said. "Just look at them and you can see the movie's title: '*The mummy returns to the moors*'," and then I laughed sardonically.

"Stop it," Friede said with reproach.

"You're right; that was impolite." I grew quiet because I knew I was only making fun of them and their leather beaten faces because I was afraid that their fate awaited me.

It was obvious that by the way the old ones nodded and winked at each other or said, "You alright?" that they had known each other for decades. There was also a familial glint of light that beamed from their eyes as they spoke to one another. They talked of nothing that was remotely interesting to me or understandable to Friede, but to them it was profound and immediate.

It was about their life from sun up to sundown in mundane villages around their county. I imagined that neither war nor peace had altered their pattern of life since the industrial revolution. Each day would have always been surrounded by a never ceasing toil to the lords of the land.

These old folks may have sacrificed their youth to either the land or the loom, but they had not relinquished their pride in survival. The timbre of their accents told me that they were children of the rough and ready north. Each vowel, consonant, or cough dripped as if it were resin from a gnarled oak tree that had weathered a millennium of storms on some forsaken moor.

It was hard for Friede to comprehend what the other riders on the bus said because they spoke with the speed of rabbits in a cadence unfamiliar to her ears. She might not have grasped their words, but she did notice them frequently look over to her as if she were an orange in a sack of potatoes.

"Why do they stare at me so?" she asked.

"It is nothing. They are just not used to seeing someone like you on a bus going to Halifax."

To hide from them, Friede snuggled close to my shoulder, and I tried to reassure her. "Forget them," I said, "because you will see a hundred more like them where we are going."

"I will?" she said with curiosity.

"Yes. We are now in the north, and the counties are full of characters that could not breathe anywhere else but in Yorkshire," I said.

"We have people like that, too, in Germany," she said, trying to draw similarities between our two countries. "For example," Friede continued, "look at the Altona district of Hamburg. Everyone there is independent, crass, and brazen. They speak a different dialect of German and don't take kindly to blowhards."

I agreed but added, "In Yorkshire, it is like nothing has changed in two hundred years and nothing will change for two hundred more. My grandfather wouldn't feel out of place in 1948 Halifax, even though he was born in 1841."

"Then why did we come here?" she pointedly asked me.

"It is a way station, a place to get our feet wet and see what fate brings us," I said. "Besides, Germany is a mess right now. It has no prospects for someone like you or me at the moment. The only people making a decent living in your country are the spivs because they turn a profit on the misery of others. For now, it is better that I try my luck up in the north, where at least I have a few friends that I can rely upon. But don't worry because we have each other, and that is all we need to be happy in Halifax."

Friede smiled, but her eyes remained uncertain of my promise of happiness in the wilds of West Yorkshire.

I looked away from Friede and over to the old pensioners. They bounced around on the bus without complaint. *Those are the people I come from*, I thought, and it didn't matter how much I wished otherwise; the north was in my blood. I both loved and hated Yorkshire and its people. I admired their strength of character, their sense of humour that could divert the devil but never convert him against his handy work. I respected their bullock stubborn strength of belief, and I despised their compliancy at being downtrodden. I detested their willingness to take second best or their casual acceptances that some were just destined to lose and others win. It seemed that they all knew the game of life was fixed from the get go, so it was better to laugh at your situation because crying wasn't going to get you anything more in this world but a wet handkerchief.

On the way, I started to tell Friede more about my past than I had ever dared to tell her when we dated in Germany. It was a tough

59

go, and I stopped after I recounted that my family was so poor that as a boy I pillaged rubbish bins located in back alleys behind restaurants to feed my sister and myself. It was like trying to describe the colour blue to the blind. I was also petrified that the more I revealed about my history, the more she would come to regret our marriage.

"Go on," she said when she noticed me stumble as I told her about my boyhood. Her eyes were filled with empathy, but I couldn't continue. I was afraid that I would break down and weep. So I did what Yorkshire men do best when there are no words to explain their anger or pain: I made her laugh with a silly song.

It was late in afternoon by the time our bus struggled like an asthmatic up Boothtown Road. I looked outside the window of our bus and watched the clouds curl around the sun like a cat looking for comfort near a fireplace. I nudged Friede and told her we were almost there.

"Look," I said and pointed out the window to All Soul's Church. It was where the well-to-do worshipped God and the common worker lived in the shadow of its impressive spires.

"Does your family go there on Sunday?" she asked.

I laughed and said, "My family has had little schooling, but we discovered early on that if there was a God, He was not to be found in the churches of Yorkshire. But we made up for our lack of belief with cleanliness by frequenting the public baths located close to the church."

"There is no bath at your mother's house?" Friede asked.

I apologised and said, "Sorry, luv, all she's got is a tin tub, like everyone else around us."

"No one on the street has a bath?" Friede asked as if she were in school inquiring about a primitive society.

"No bath or privy," I said.

"What?" she exclaimed.

"In the north," I said, "the majority of the people have outdoor toilets. The ones that have an indoor privy are well to do and have a full bib and tucker. I am afraid Britain is not like Germany, or even the rest of Western Europe where pretty well everyone has an indoor WC. Your Hitler was a mean bugger," I said, "but he was good for modern sanitation."

Friede looked at me with momentary anger and responded, "Don't say such foolish things. Hitler gave us nothing but misery and nightmares. The Nazis only brought destruction to my country."

"Sure," I said and changed the topic. "At least Ackroyd Park is nearby. I can tell you, most working class homes do not have a finer park in their local area."

I explained to Friede that the park was formerly a large Victorian estate that had been turned into a museum and garden. "I used to go there quite often as a lad to read a book and escape my family."

When we passed the chemist shop, I said to Friede that our stop was next. She stood and moved to the exit while I followed with our bags. When the bus pulled away, it left us in a haze of diesel fumes. I waited for a moment on the kerb, not daring to move, and Friede asked why I had stopped. "Catching my breath," I said with a harrowed smile like a man ready to take the thirteen steps to the gallows. "I'm just getting my bearings."

When we reached the front door of my mother's terraced house, I hesitated. I looked down at the cheap suit the RAF had provided me and thought, *You look like a bloody DP, just fresh from a refugee camp*, whereas Friede looked beautiful. I feared she was almost too rare an item to be brought indoors to the world of my mother. Friede noticed my hesitation and said, "Why don't you ring the doorbell?"

"In this neighbourhood," I replied, "there are no doorbells."

"Why not" Friede asked?

I laughed. "Generally, the only regular visitors on this street are the debt collectors or the police, and they don't need a bell to announce their visit. If you want to get someone's attention on Boothtown Road, give the door a good thrashing."

"Watch," I said, then banged on the door with my open palm and yelled out that it was the milk man.

Even though she knew we were arriving that day, my mother opened her door with suspicion and restrained hostility. She seemed to sniff the air around her to determine if I was friend or foe. At first my mother's appearance startled Friede, and she moved closer to me as if a giant dog had jumped out at her. As I observed my mother's looming figure before us, I thought, *Bugger, the jig is up.*

I shuffled nervously on my feet as my mother stood arms akimbo before us. My mother had aged since my last visit the year previous.

61

In her youth, my mother Lillian was considered a beauty, but ill fortune, poverty, and too many children with different fathers had taken their toll on her looks. Nearing fifty-five, she was now only able to turn a man's head by the cut of her remarks rather than by her once pretty face.

Lillian was as tall and domineering as ever, and she blocked our entrance way to the house with her body. Her hair was streaked with grey and combed tightly back into a bun. Her dress hung around her like a cloth thrown over an oversized dining room table. The flower pattern on her dress was as faded as her youth; both had vanished in a cold wash, scrubbed away with carbolic soap. My mum looked at me first, and then over to Friede, whereupon her thick, dark eyebrows arched like Mephistopheles after his expulsion from Heaven.

My mother's blunt expression depicted both pleasure at my arrival and mordant amusement that I was in need of her help. I had seen that look so many times before that I once remarked that my mother was a Yorkshire version of Janus, the god of beginnings and endings. "It all starts out sunshine and roses and turns to shite by Tuesday with my ma."

There was a layer of red lipstick on her thin lips that made her first words appear to foam with blood. "Blimey, Bill, look what the cat dragged in." She was addressing her aging lover that had replaced my dad long ago as both irresolute bread winner and life partner. He was wedged up behind her like a cow in the back of a knackers' van. I heard from behind, my mother and Bill, my two younger half-brothers snicker at my mother's remark.

"Hi ya mum," I said with latent anger. "This is my wife, Friede."

Lillian's mood changed, and she beamed friendliness and motherly charm. In a tone reserved for creditors, my mother said to Friede, "Come in, lass. You must be plum tired after such a long journey from Manchester to humble Halifax."

Lillian pulled Friede into the house with so much force that Bill and my brothers, who were crammed up behind her, scurried out of the way like mice avoiding a cat. My mother led Friede into the kitchen and pushed her into a seat with a strong hand.

Bill Moxon looked at me and said, "I'll be buggered - you are the last person I expected back under this roof."

"You can say that again, Bill," I replied.

Friede's face was flush from the confusion of meeting everyone at once. Friede tried to express her gratitude at meeting my mother, and instead of saying thank you reverted to German and said, "*Danke.*"

Lillian stopped her fussing and said - like the wolf to Red Riding Hood - "You've got a strange accent, luv, but that's wot comes from being a bloody foreigner."

I was about to protest when my mother blustered at me.

"Oi, lad, it's good to see thee looking so well. You must have grown an inch or so since I last saw you," my mother said with a laugh.

"You look well, too, mum," I said with a bit of irritation in my voice.

"Ta, son, but my ruddy cheeks hide many a complaint. It's been a hard war on all of us, and they tell uz it's done and dusted. But how do you know it's over when we still have all this bleeding rationing? It's been tough to make ends meet and nothing is getting any easier. Now, I know you've just got yer feet in the door, but don't be mucking your mother about."

"What are you talking about, mum?" I asked. I was confused about where she was leading me in this conversation.

"Don't be daft, lad, you know what tomorrow is. So you better ave it for me because I am not the bleeding Salvation Army."

"What in the blazes are you talking about, mum?" I said with growing irritation.

"The coin, lad, because tomorrow is rent day, and it's best thou does not forget to honour thy mother," she said and rubbed her thumb and forefinger together. "It is common knowledge that brass doesn't grow on any tree near or far from Boothtown Road."

"Christ," I said, "you will never change, mum. You are like the bloody ferry man across the river Styx."

"Wot?" said my mother,

"You are a bloody miser," I said.

"Had to be," said my mother defensively, "with you lot like kittens looking for milk. Somebody had to provide."

"Didn't stop you going out on the piss every Friday, while Mary and I were back at home, cold and hungry."

63

At this point, Bill interjected and said, "You two are like a bloody dog and cat. Now go on and both shut it. We've got a visitor in this ouse."

I looked over at Friede, and she looked as white as a ghost. I walked over to her and stroked her shoulder, and in a calmer tone I said to my mother, "I have your money, but I won't promise how long we'll be staying put."

"It better be for a while because we did up the attic right and proper for you and your Jerry bride," Lillian said in a belligerent tone.

"Mum," I hollered, "for Christ sake, don't call her that."

"Sorry," my mother said addressing Friede. "I meant no offense to thee. "We just never had a German staying under our roof before today."

"I thought you've never had someone from York in your house either, but you'd probably take them to be the enemy as well."

Somehow, a truce was declared between me and my mother, who then ordered my brother Matt to bring out a plate of sandwiches.

"Got them fresh this morning from Grosvenor's," she said proudly. Matt placed them onto the table like chub being dropped into the ocean for a shark feeding frenzy.

In the middle of the table rested a thin, ornate, but empty fruit bowl. It had been a gift to my mother from Friede. I had brought it to her on my last leave from Germany. My mother noticed Friede staring at the delicate bowl amidst the indelicacies of my mother's household. With her mouth full of roast pork, Lillian said to Friede, "That be war booty. My Harry scoffed it from Germany for me."

"It was a gift," I declared wearily. Suddenly, Bill Moxon opened a couple bottles of stout and poured a glass for everyone.

Lillian, with a note of resignation in her voice, said, "It's good to see you back home with your German wife."

We sat around the table for another thirty minutes, eating and drinking while my family stared at Friede as if I had brought the Empress of China to kip. Finally, Bill said it was time for his bed because "they start you early at the Cat's Eye factory down road."

"How's that working for you?" I asked.

"Pay's not grand, but it's steady, honest labour that will see me through until I am in the ground," he said confidently.

My mother added, "It's the only place that will keep him 'cause of his bloody temper."

"Lil," moaned Bill but stopped before he started a row with her.

"Aye," I said, "it is time we retired, too. It's been a long day, and I want to get an early start in the morning to look for work."

Chapter Nine:
In morning's clear light:

Despite the years since I had been under my mother's dominion, one night under her roof confirmed to me that tranquillity was still not a frequent visitor to her home on Boothtown Road. It was impossible for repose to take root in the squat terraced houses of Britain. Peace was not possible in these communities for workers which were no more than marshalling yards for human animals. The homes on Boothtown Road were just uncomfortable places to lay your head and rest between shifts at the forge, mill, or mine. These estates crammed as many living souls as possible into the smallest space, and the landlords said *be thankful to your God and your country that you've got a roof over thy head.*

They were not constructed for a life of contemplation or quiet reflection. Discomfort was incorporated into the design. It made sure the occupants were never able to relax or get a moment alone. *It keeps them keen for work* was the landlords' mantra when they erected these match stick hovels across England's hills and dales.

Before we crept upstairs to our bed, my mother said, "Lad, take this," and she handed me a lit candle that rested in a clay holder.

Friede looked at it with curiosity until I explained that the loft was not equipped with electric or gas light.

"It is dark as coal up in that attic," said one of my brothers while the other one warned Friede to mind the ghost. "He's a friendly one but a loud bugger at night, especially when he drags his chain about and moans 'cause he's got stomach ache."

"Shut it," I said and glared at them like an irritated, embarrassed older brother.

Wagging her finger at me, my mother said, "Buy your own light for tomorrow night because we are not running a hotel for thee here."

To get to our cramped room, we had to walk up to the second floor landing. At the back was a door that led to a set of narrow stairs that took us up to our minute, tight, airless bedroom. The candle's light was enough for me to see that my mother hadn't been able to do much with the limited space. It looked like a cluttered, insignificant storage closet. Our bed was stuck in the middle of the loft, while its headboard was pushed up against the interior wall. There was a night stand that looked like it had been bought at a gypsy market. On the wall opposite the bed, my mother had placed a dressing table with a mirror and wash basin on its surface.

"Come," I said to Friede while I pushed away our luggage that my brothers had hauled up after tea.   I placed the candle on the dressing table.

Friede wrapped her arms around herself and lamented, "It is so cold up here."

"I am sorry," I said, "but the damn house has only one fireplace. It is in that cubby hole my mother calls a parlour. There is no other heat in this place but the stove in the kitchen. It is probably best if you throw your coat on top of our blanket before you go to sleep."

Suddenly, a draft began to drift from the floor boards, and it made the candle light flicker. Friede grabbed her night clothes and said, "I am going to change underneath the bed covers. At least I won't die of frostbite there."

I tried to laugh it off as she slipped into the tiny antiquated bed.

While throwing her clothes off and putting on her nightgown, Friede said, "I am glad I used the outdoor toilet before we got up here."

I didn't bother getting into the bed to undress. I was used to cold attics because I had lived in too many of them as a boy. Something else prevented me from getting comfortable: I didn't want to admit to Friede that I knew that this was a miserable, damp night chamber. While I pulled my trousers off and folded them into neat creases, Friede started to laugh.

"What have I done now?" I said self-consciously until I noticed that the candle light had cast a deformed silhouette of my body against the squat, sloped ceiling.

"It is rather funny," she said, "that we are sleeping in the attic and your shadow looks like Quasi Moto."

I blew the candle out and jumped into the bed beside her. I said to Friede while I put my cold hands onto her bare shoulder, "Then you must be my Esmeralda."

"Sleep well, my bell ringer," she replied in a nocturnal voice. "I hope tomorrow brings some fantastic news for both of us because it

68

has been a hard day." Friede then turned her back to me and fell asleep.

I couldn't sleep, and my mind raced with anger, shame, and regret that I had ended back at my mother's home. I lay awake for a long while and stared up into the skylight and out onto the dark clouds. On the streets below, I heard dogs growl and bark as they hunted in packs for grub from unsecured trash bins. I turned to look at Friede and saw that she was wrapped up in her coat like a caterpillar in its cocoon. Her head was exposed and rested uneasily on the pillow.

She was asleep, but her face looked tense and remorseful. At times she uttered an unintelligible word in German, while at other moments her legs quaked uncontrollably as if they were being bombarded with electrical currents. I knew that her subconscious was trapped in some very rough water, where bad dreams were like a tempest to a tiny skiff. I hoped that until daylight broke and sent her back to the waking world that her imagination would steer her towards a safe cove and shelter her against anymore nightmares.

When sleep finally came for me, it took me harshly by the hand and plunged me into a trance of dreams, memories, and terrors. I floated back to my life in Germany, and for a second I felt happy but then the winds changed and I was blown back towards my childhood. There, I was overwhelmed and crushed by helplessness and despair. I awoke with a start and choked on my past as it if it were brackish water.

I was now sweaty, miserable, and wide awake because below me a discordant symphony of noise began to play from each room in our small, unhappy house. From my brother's bedroom, farts ambled to my ear like a ship's claxon in a foggy channel. They were quickly replaced by the more audible noise of my mother damning Bill Moxon who lay beside her and snored like a Cyclops.

"Bugger," I whispered and pulled a thin blanket up past my eyes. I tried to shut out the clamour around me and the trembling in my mind. Sometime before the horse drawn carts of the rag and bone men started to wend their way down the cobbled streets below, I nodded back to sleep.

I came to when my bladder told me it was sunrise, and I jumped into consciousness. Friede was still entombed in a deep slumber

69

beside me. Her face looked at peace for the first time since she had arrived in Britain.

I slipped from the bed as gently as possible and got dressed because I wanted to surprise Friede with breakfast. I decided to go up the street to the cake shop and bring something sweet back for us. I crept from the room and down the stairs, making sure that I didn't wake her.

When I got downstairs, I found Lillian in the kitchen reading an old edition of the Halifax Courier. From behind the paper, I heard her slurp her morning cuppa tea. My mother looked up from her paper and reproached me sharply. "What are you doing skulking about?"

"I'm not skulking," I replied. "I am just trying to be quiet because Friede had a rough night. I'll just pop out and fetch her some cakes from the shop up at top of the street, for us."

"She lives pretty high and mighty," responded my mother. "Who gets to have a lie in on a Thursday and served cakes? You're not a Rothschild, you know. Harry, be sensible with that lass or you'll never keep her, boy. It will be thy road to ruin."

Irritated, I said, "If I ever want directions to perdition, I'll ask you, mum, because you drew the map to ruination."

Lillian shrugged her shoulders at me and resumed sipping her tea. As the door closed behind me, my mother called out as if she were the town crier, "Don't forget thy rent for yer mum."

I left the house and muttered, "Stupid cow."

I detested my mother's bare bones sentiment towards her children. Ever since The Great Depression, poverty had scourged her heart and twisted her ability to nurture her kids. My mother had forgotten how to be tender because the world had shown her so little kindness. The only faith my mother had was that life was a disappointment, and money, unlike love, was more safe, secure, and tender than any lover or devoted child.

The cake shop was located in a single story dwelling about half a block up the road from my mother's house. Even though it was a pokey little place, the whole neighbourhood popped into the shop on their way to work for a pasty or on their way home for a piece of cake.

Somehow, the shop looked different to me than when I was last inside it in 1941. I supposed it was like everything else in Britain: its best days were long gone.

From behind the counter, a familiar voice called out, "Hello, luv. What happened to you? I haven't seen you in ages."

It was a woman named Rosie. In 1939, I had been sweet on her, but she rebuffed all my advances with a quick laugh and the same retort. "You'd break my heart, Harry. Besides, I am at least five years older than you."

"You haven't changed a bit and look as lovely as ever," I said.

"That's very sweet of you, but I feel as old as the stones they used to build Boothtown Road. What you having?" she asked, and I pointed to some Best Well cakes and a rock bun.

While she collected the cakes and put them into a box, she asked me what I had done in the war. I told her I had been in the RAF.

"Flyboy?" she asked.

I laughed and responded. "Not bloody likely. I was a wireless OP with my feet firmly on the ground."

"What you've been up to since we gave Hitler the sack?"

I told her I had been stationed in Germany.

"Oi, aye, you're a real globe trotter."

"Too right," I said. "I even got married."

"Go on," she said. "I am so pleased for you. Your lass did all right for herself when she caught a man as good as you."

I beamed because that was the first compliment I'd heard in a long while.

"It's not someone from round here, I bet?"

"No, you got that right. It's a German girl. I met her in Hamburg. How about you, I inquired.

"There's no man in my life. Haven't had a fella who was sweet on me since the war and that bugger left me with a little nipper," she said without rancour.

I wasn't sure how to respond when Rosie interrupted my uncoordinated silence.

"It's not as bad as that. It's not like he died or anything. He just did a runner and went back to his wife after the war. It serves me right for trusting an officer to be a bleeding gentleman."

She wiped her hands on a grey smock and produced a picture of a little boy. "He's the only one that's got my heart now."

As I was about to leave the shop, Rosie called out and asked where I was living.

"Back with my mother," I responded.

"Bugger you, back in the arms of Ma Moxon. I don't fancy your chances or your missus surviving your mum when she is on a tear."

I agreed and said I was going to start looking straight away for a new set of rooms.

"Good luck," she said. "There is nowt to find from Bradford to Liverpool. You would think that the Germans had bombed all of the north to the ground like Dresden. Not for money or love can anyone find a decent room in this town."

I agreed.

"Oi ya" she said as an afterthought, "the only place which I know of being available is cross street."

Rosie pointed out the window, and I turned to see what she was talking about.

Shocked, I said, "You mean Fat Annie is taking in lodgers?"

Rosie replied, "Too right. She's looking for a resident to live in her cellar. Do you remember her, Harry?"

"She was unforgettable," I said, "but nobody in the area could recall a time when Annie hadn't lived on Boothtown Road. Nobody knew her age or bothered to find out what her last name was; she was just fat Annie because she weighed more than twenty stone and wore workman's overalls."

"Does she still sit outside her front door like an Easter Island stone statue?" I enquired.

"Have a look when you go out of the shop; she'll be there until doomsday. During the war, everyone started to say she was our air raid warden because she never went inside. 'Annie, have you seen any Henkels today?' was what everyone said when they walked by her."

"Didn't she have a son?" I asked.

"Poor dim witted Eddie is still her faithful stoop companion. Nothing ever changes on Boothtown Road," Rosie said with a laugh.

"Do you know that the school kids sing the same song about Annie when you wuz a lad? 'Oi, there's Big Fat Annie, why don't ya bend over to show us yer dirty black fanny.'"

"I bet they'll be singing until your own boy is an old man," I said, haunted by the fact that the road was always going to filled with castaways from life.

When I got back to my mother's house, I found Friede downstairs in the scullery. She was washing dishes while my mother rested comfortably on her chair and chatted with Friede.

"Yer Friede," said my mother "was just telling me about the house you had in Germany. I set her straight about what you can get in Halifax on a worker's wages. I told her to put aside any fancy notions of a house on a worker's wages in this town. The best you two can hope for and got is that snug room upstairs."

"Mam, can you give it a rest?" I said as I kissed Friede on the cheek and pulled her away from the wash sink. I then said to her, "Don't let my mother boss you about, and remember, you are not her unpaid domestic."

"I don't mind doing the dishes," Friede said. "It gave me something to do while you were out. I want to be useful because I know I am not on holidays."

"Too right- a lass has got to be useful in this world because men are good for bloody nothing," my mother said.

I put the cakes on the table and made Friede eat something while my mother looked on, irritated that I hadn't offered her anything.

While Friede ate her breakfast, I handed our rent money over to my mother.

She eagerly grabbed the coins and counted them down to the last penny. After she had finished doing her sums, my mother opened up her ledger book. With a stubby, thick pencil, she turned to a fresh page and noted the amount she had received from me.

"Son, you're alright now until the next time, and look how much you are saving, living with your mum."

I am not saving anything living with you, I thought and started to gauge how much money I still had in reserve. I figured that I had enough money from my RAF pay to live without work for a month, but if nothing turned up by then, things would start to become difficult. It was essential that I start to look for work immediately. There was no doubt in my mind that I also had to find us a new place to live before my mother ruined my marriage with her sarcasm, pessimism, and distrust of everyone.

"What do you two have planned today?" inquired my mother with no particular interest in the answer.

"Going out," I said while under my breath I grumbled, "to find a new place to live."

Just before we left, I told my mother that I planned to visit my sister Mary at her house on Low Moor as soon as possible.

"Don't bother," said Lillian.

"Why not?" I asked, growing irritated with my mother.

"I forgot to tell you, your sister's in a bad way with her man again." My mother's mouth scowled in disgust as she contemplated my sister's marriage and perhaps her own failed relationships. She then spit out, "He's a fine piece of work, a bolter to the Army and bolter to his family. So, she's not up for seeing company because like us all, she's in the shit."

Shortly afterwards, I left the house with Friede to look for new accommodations.

Chapter Ten:
It is the work house for thee

The front door of my mother's house closed with a thud. Outside, I heard birdsong from Ackroyd Park. Above us, the sky was cloudless and coloured in a light blue wash. There was a slight breeze, which carried in its draft the smoke and the stench from the weaving and carpet mills and blew it out onto the sparse moors that surrounded Halifax. Even the familiar reek of sweet confectionary that belched from the giant smoke stacks attached to the Macintosh factory had drifted away from the town like a fog of toffee. It felt like spring, and I was able to smell fresh blossoms in the air.

Friede linked her arm in mine and said, "It feels good to be out of your mother's house and that stuffy attic. I was beginning to feel like I was trapped inside a shipping trunk."

"A nice walk is what the doctor ordered to blow the stink off," I said light-heartedly.

"So what is our plan?" Friede asked.

"Explore Halifax," I responded, "because this is going to be our home for some time, and I want you to become familiar with the surroundings."

Friede agreed that it was a good idea. "I don't want to be a stranger here; I want to know Halifax as well as Hamburg."

People's Park was our first destination. It had been created by James Paxton, who had also designed the Crystal Palace for Queen Victoria's Jubilee. Why Halifax had been honoured with this little patch of imperialistic landscape architecture was a mystery to me.

Some said the park was a gift to the people of Halifax and a reminder that our empire was civilized, strong, and vibrant. It seemed to me that despite the Park's charm, it demonstrated more the divide between the classes than anything else.

Friede and I entered the park through the Faux Roman Column entrance. Once inside, we walked down a gravel path that criss-crossed the manicured lawns in geometrical precision. On both side of us, Roman porticos and well-maintained flower beds competed for attention with statues of once prominent men of girth and financial stature.

Friede pointed to them and asked who they had been.

"Fat buggers, now dead," I said, "but when alive, they lined their pockets in commerce or in government."

Evenly spaced throughout the park were marble fountains that sprayed cold Yorkshire water into the air as if it were Fontainebleau. At the park's epicentre was a smartly painted band shell. It was here on Saturday evenings that brass orchestras entertained weekend strollers with Gilbert and Sullivan tunes.

Despite being too grand for its city, too Victorian for the 1940s, and too full of its own self-importance, People's Park was still remarkably beautiful and serene. I smiled at Friede and said wistfully, "I shouldn't like this park, but I do. During the Depression, I found refuge here from all the ugliness and desperation that brewed in my house and in my neighbourhood."

"This will be a lovely spot for us to have a picnic on a hot summer's day," Friede remarked.

It didn't seem prudent to disappoint Friede by telling her that a heat wave in Halifax was as rare as sighting Hailey's comet, so I quickly changed the subject. "People's Park may look posh and opulent during the day, but on a Saturday night, it is chock o' bloc with randy teenagers. When I was a lad, there was so much lovemaking going on down in the thickets that those old statues on their pedestals must have wanted to jump down and chase away the sex struck kids of Halifax."

"When it is springtime, it is the same all across the world," Friede responded. "It doesn't matter if it's Asia or Europe, young men and women need to find comfort in each other's arms." Friede brushed away some hair that had fallen across her face and teasingly asked, "Were you one of those lads who kissed his girl in the park on Saturday night?"

I laughed and replied, "Not as often as I wished."

"Why not" Friede asked?

"I learned early on that you get only so far with quoting a sonnet from Wordsworth to a girl from the Calder Valley. A Halifax girl is practical lass, and nobody's fool. She wants to exchange her kisses for a ring, a registry marriage, and a fortnight at Blackpool every summer. I thought my kisses were worth more than a brass penny life, and besides, most of them didn't think my dreams were worth tuppence."

Friede held my hand and said reassuringly, "For me, your dreams are worth their weight in gold."

Friede kissed me on the lips, and then we walked silently along the path until we reached an ornate sculpture. At that point, we moved onto the grass and let a train of young mothers who were perambulating their infants stroll past us. The noise from the squeaking wheels of their metal prams sounded like a slow moving locomotive.

"The girls of yesteryear," I said mournfully to Friede.

I wondered to myself if those mothers began their sexual life in the park, like so many other teenagers from this city. Had they, like the girls I'd known in my youth, made love to the lads who lived down their lane? Were these the same girls who, in a flush of passion, made love to their beaus underneath the trees or behind the shrubbery and cooed out, "Da ya really mean it when you say ya luv me, or are you just taking the piss"?

Did they ever find out the answer to their question? I wasn't sure if they wanted to know the answer now. Something greater and more terrible had happened to everyone in the world, and now the answers to their questions were more complex than "Is his heart true?"

We sat for a time on a bench and enjoyed the sun against our faces and relived our happier times in Hamburg. Noticing that the day was getting on, I suggested we finish our journey by looking for a new place to live.

Soon afterwards, we left the park and moved in the direction of the town's High Street and closer to the Council buildings. During our walk we passed by many residences, some grand, some in decay, and others in need of government condemnation. However, we were not fortunate to find any that were looking for lodgers.

After a while, we reached the entrance to a back alley that ran off Gibbet Street. It was a short cut to Commercial Street. After we were on it, I realised it would have been wiser to have taken a longer route to the city centre. The road probably hadn't changed much since the days when Queen Anne reigned over the island. The buildings on either side of the street appeared to collapse onto the roadway like a disembowelled prisoner.

Looking around at the destitution, I warned Friede to be careful. "Watch your step here," I said cautiously as I grabbed her arm and brought her closer to me.

Friede moved on the broken cobblestone street like a sleepwalking child. Overwhelmed by curiosity, she let go of my hand and walked towards a warren whose window was wide open. Inside the building, Friede looked at a jumble of poverty; rubbish, broken furniture, and children in dirty clothing. Suddenly, a greasy woman's head jumped out from the open window and screeched, "Fancy anything, luv? It's all on sale today."

Friede, confused and ashamed by her inquisitiveness, shyly replied, "No, thank you."

The slum dweller spit onto the road, and with a voice that sounded as if she gargled with nails said, "Well, seeing that yer not buying, luv, you best fuck off home." She spat again and said in warning, "If you come down this road way again, I'll clout you till yer brains run down the side of your head."

"That's enough!" I screamed at the slag, who hadn't seen a good scrub brush since she was washed at birth. I grabbed Friede's arm and dragged her back towards me.

"Come on," I said. We then hurriedly walked away from the street and the woman who had been made a lunatic from poverty and gin.

It was a relief for me to get out of the derelict road and on to Commercial Street.

"See," I said to Friede, "this is an alright street with proper shops and people who are not down in the gutter."

"It wasn't the woman's fault," Friede replied. "It was mine for thinking she was like an exhibit at a museum. But I am still glad to be out of there. I hope you don't have any more scary places to show me."

"No. I am just going to take you to the Arcade because Grosvenor Grocers have a shop inside and I used to work there before the war. Someone there might know about a job for me or a room to let for us."

"Didn't you used to be one of the managers at the shop?" Friede asked.

"Yes, before the war, but the owner was a devout Christadelphian; he was a follower of both God and manna. You know he even promised me that once, '*the shooting was over, there be thy smock and as before thy same job at Grosvenor's for you.*'"

"So why didn't he give you your old position back?"

I laughed sarcastically and said, "Because like most of the religious malarkey the owner spouted, it was gobshite. My place was filled with a conscientious objector named Bob who was also a member of his church. After the war he said there was nothing he could do for me. My position was no longer available."

One of the shop girls recognized me the moment we walked into Grosvenor's because we had dated briefly before the war.

"Hello, Sylvia," I said sheepishly and thought how feverishly infatuations came and went. I couldn't think why I had ever been so enamoured by her when I was a teen.

She asked me what I had been up to, but when I began to tell her, she seemed to be current with all my activities.

"How did you know I was married?" I asked.

"Word gets around like lightning in Halifax," she said.

"Do they know that I am looking for work and a place to live for Friede and me?" I said jokingly.

"That's a tall order," answered Sylvia. "I'd love to help, but there is nothing going here, and as for flats, there is nothing to be found out there. Pop in again next week because maybe things will have changed."

"Don't worry," I said with pride. "We'll be alright. I've got lots of irons in the fire."

To show me that she had not been idle, Silvia thrust her hand and dangled a finger with a wedding band wrapped tightly around it.

"Good for you," I said. "And who is the lucky man?"

"Bob, the manager," she said with confused pleasure.

"I should have guessed," I replied and didn't finish my thoughts about conscientious objections.

Silvia looked over towards Friede and said, "Harry, she looks as lovely as a ray of sunshine; pity she's only got rainy old Halifax to look forward to." When we were about to leave, Silvia asked me if we wanted to meet up later for a drink at a pub. I declined and said, "I thought your sect was against the demon drink?"

79

"I am still a sinner," she said.

Outside of the shop, I noticed that Friede looked frustrated. I asked her if everything was alright. She was quiet for a moment, as if translating her thoughts from German into English. "I know you are doing the best you can, but you wrote me all the time when I was in Germany. You never said it was going to be like this. I thought most things had been worked out before I left Hamburg."

"I don't understand," I said defensively.

"I am not complaining," she said, then became silent.

"Out with it," I said impatiently. I knew that I was at fault and that I had omitted much about life in the north and my true circumstances, but in my defence, I had believed that our landing in Halifax was going to be a smoother ride.

Frustrated and playing with her wedding ring, Friede continued. "I just didn't expect all of these family complications. I thought you and your mother got along better, and you don't. I have only been under her roof one night, and I can feel the anger, the hatred that you have for her. I can also feel the anger and dislike she has for me. And it is not only her; your brothers stare at me as if I am a zoo animal."

"She doesn't like anyone, not even me," I said. "I don't hate her, but sometimes I despise her for never saying sorry for what she did when we were young. Maybe she had no choice, I don't know, but she could just say sorry to my sister and I for making us live the way we did. As for my brothers, they have never, ever met anyone like you before in their lives, so they find you exotic; it will pass soon enough with them."

Friede didn't look satisfied with my answer. She started to probe deeper into the broken parts of my family as if she were examining a wrecked car to see what had caused it to lose control and maim its passengers.

"No, it is different. Your mother dislikes me in a very particular way." Friede then related to me that while I was out buying cakes that morning, my mother referred to her as Harry's *bit of war booty*. It made Friede feel as if she were being vilified for being from over there, the land of jack boots and iron crosses.

"My mother is an ignorant cow," I said. "If you had come from Scotland, she would have thought your arrival in Halifax was compensation for the Union. Unfortunately, she can't help it. My mum resents anyone that gets a taste of happiness because she thinks all of hers were stolen by men, the government, and my real dad's family. Look," I said, putting my arm around her shoulder. "We will be out of there soon enough because I am sure the local council, if no one else, will provide a flat to a Demobbed RAF man."

"I don't know," Friede said. "I don't know anything at all because this is not my country and I am a stranger here, dependent on my husband to keep me safe."

She looked terrified, as if all her fears about leaving home were coming true. Friede started to look more like a small animal trapped in the headlights of an oncoming vehicle than a confident young woman. After we got to the council and met with a clerk that was responsible for housing, her apprehension grew worse because it looked like the local government wasn't going to help us find lodgings either.

When I asked if there was any housing available, the expression on the clerk's face displayed a wry amusement, as if I'd requested lunch with the Lord Mayor.

I was handed an index card and told to "fill out your particulars, and if anything becomes available, we'll contact you."

"But we need something now," I said, exasperated by his officious indifference.

"Well, bugger me," responded the clerk. "We all need something now, but to get it, you need to put your name on the bleeding waiting list, and then hop into the queue."

"Right," I said, scribbling down my mother's address. "And how long will it take to hear back from someone?"

The clerk informed me that the list for housing was as long as the road to London.

"You should have come sooner," he said.

"I was in the services."

"So was everyone," he remarked, "and some of them came a lot quicker than you. It is very late in the day to be looking for housing because the council's skint and there is no money for building new estates. We're not on the Marshall plan, you know like France or Germany. In Britain, everyone has got to keep buggering on, or that's what they tell us at any rate."

"All right, all right," I said, trying to shut him up. "But how long will all of this take?"

Without hesitation, he said like a tailor who knows a man's inseam just by seeing him walk into his shop, "From where you are today to the top of the list, two years, give or take a day."

I pleaded with him that I needed something right away.

He leaned towards me as if he were giving me a tip on the races and said, "The best I can offer is a few nights in the work house. Mind you, it will mean separate dormitories for you and the missus because men are housed far away from the women, for obvious reasons," he said in a conspiratorial manner.

The moment he mentioned the work house, Friede's eyes grew bright with fear and humiliation. She whispered, "Dickens," as if it were a curse.

"Not as bad as that, luv," said the clerk. "The work house has improved since the days of Oliver Twist."

We left the council offices, and I began to swear at the sodding council, the sodding north, the sodding country, and the sodding RAF. Friede started to cry in confusion at my anger and our predicament.

I lit two cigarettes and handed her one, hoping to calm her down and restore her shattered illusions, but she waved the fag away. I crushed out the burning heater with my thumb and forefinger and shoved the Players back into its pack.

"Come on," I said, "let's get out of here."

Friede and I slowly began to walk home, dejected and beaten. We were walking down Commercial Street when a voice called out from the throng of pedestrians, "Oi, over here, Harry."

I looked around and saw a man in a fashionable raincoat and stylish Fedora. It was Eric Whitley, a boyhood chum who had on his arm Dorothy Butterworth. She was the elder sister of Doug, another one of my childhood friends.

I quickly explained to Friede that these were old friends of mine, then we rushed over to them.

Eric took one look at Friede and said, "Looks like you're doing alright for yourself, Harry."

"You don't look so bad yourself, Eric," I replied.

Dorothy jumped in and said to me, "Before you get the wrong idea, Harry, Eric is being a real gent and taking a lady down on her luck for lunch."

"Better yet," said Eric, "Why don't you two come to lunch with us?"

"I don't know," I said, looking at my watch as if we had somewhere else to go. In truth, I was worried about wasting my cash reserve on a meal. Eric sensed my reluctance and guessed it was about money. Being short of the ready was something Eric didn't have to worry about, as he had been in selective service throughout the war. He was a tool and die maker who had made a pretty bundle on side jobs. He threw out a wicked grin at Friede and said, "I've got a smashing idea: let lunch be my treat. Call it paying a debt to one of our air aces returning to Civvy Street."

"Where should we have lunch?" I asked.

"We'll go out with a bang today and dine at the White Swan."

Chapter Eleven:
The White Swan and the Black Albatross of Boothtown

The White Swan Hotel was constructed by the local carpet magnet John Crossley at the beginning of Queen Victoria's long reign. He made his fortune by producing machine made carpets that were sold all through Britain's dominions and colonies. Crossley was a man of his times and saw no contradiction in being a capitalist who enslaved thousands of workers to a life of serfdom and also a philanthropist that built schools and established scholarships for the poor. It was the creed of the nineteenth century that a true Christian was both rapacious in greed and munificent in charity.

His hotel was erected in the grand manner of his day and would not have been out of place in fashionable London or the more mercantile Manchester. Crossley wanted visitors to recognize not only his wealth and power but that Halifax was not a mere provincial outpost; it was a city that contributed to the nation's wealth and prosperity.

In 1948, Halifax had been humbled by the twentieth century but not the White Swan. The hotel still stood proud against the rest of the soot-stained edifices that populated Princess Street. The building's facade looked defiant and opulent to me. It was as if it refused to accept this century or the blandness of post-war Britain. Inside that building, I thought it was like another country, or at the very least an oasis for those with money who wanted to ignore the regular world and its ration book diet.

"It's been ages since I was here," I said to Eric.

"I'm a regular now," replied Eric.

"I haven't been inside since I was granted leave during the war," I said.

"When were you on leave?" Eric asked in a peeved manner. "Why didn't you bother to look me up for a drink?"

"I didn't have time," I said apologetically. "I was in Halifax for, probably, less than forty-eight hours. It was right after I had completed my induction and finished my wireless training."

"When I got back to Halifax after being square bashed I was really filled with piss and vinegar. I marched into the bar room thinking I was finally the cat's whiskers. I wanted to show myself off to all those toffee-nosed squires who ran the town and show them what a serving RAF man looks like in uniform."

"They probably didn't even bat an eye when they saw you coming in," said Eric.

"No," I said with a laugh. "The barman didn't care, as long as I had the coin for my beer."

"What about the businessmen?" Eric asked.

"I don't think they even bothered to look up from their drinks to get a whiff of me. I was as important to them as the minions who toiled in their factories. We were just commodities to them, like coal or wheat things that are bought and sold to make them profit."

Eric held the door open for us, and we walked nonchalant through the expansive hotel entrance and into the drinks room. The chandeliers suspended from the ceiling cast a bright electric light down towards us. Dorothy pointed to the walls, which were decorated with replica Georgian paintings that depicted the life of English gentleman, and said, "They really do think a lot of themselves in here, don't they?"

"Look," I added, "even the windows are frosted so nobody on the outside will rub their nose against them to see how the other half lives."

Our lunch that afternoon was simple but elegant. We ate an assortment of finger sandwiches, which were presented to us on a tiered silver tray. We drank Heineken, which was pulled fresh from a barrel located in a cellar below the rail of the bar. It was served to us in tall, chilled, sculpted glasses. A perfect head of beer rested just over the lip of the glass, which foamed with the aroma of hops and barley. Eric asked us if we had ever tasted a better beer.

Friede said that her native city was famed for its beer cellars and waterfront cafes.

I then leaned over towards Eric, and said "Once, I tasted Heineken so fresh, you would have thought it was milk from a farm."

"Where was that?" he asked in disbelief.

"In Den Hague, during the war," I responded boastfully.

Eric looked a little disappointed by my response, so I remarked, "But I have never tasted a better beer in Halifax."

My retort cheered Eric up enough for him to talk about what he loved most: himself. He began to tell us about his war and what a fortunate experience it was for him

"It was a cracking good time for me. Blimey, the money I made. If there is ever a bust up between us and the Russians, I'll be on easy street," he said confidently.

During Eric's tale of war-time profit, Friede had a courteous expression drawn across her face, as if she were listening to a not-so-amusing story from an employer. It was only if you looked directly into her eyes that you could see that she was displeased by his selfish outlook on the war. She didn't like my friend's civilian bravado, and for a moment I thought she was going to tell him so.

It was at that point I thought it best to interrupt Eric's flowing account of pounds and pence by saying, "I am satisfied with just being part of the one war. I don't think we need another. The RAF paid me well enough for what they asked of me. Besides, I didn't fall into anything dangerous. So I am satisfied, even if I am now in this leaky life boat called Britain."

Eric look at his frosted beer glass and said, "You're right; we don't need any more of that. Besides, at my work we are just as busy as if the war were still on."

"Have you heard anything, lately, from Roy?" I asked him.

I explained to Friede that Roy was our mutual friend from boyhood. During the war, he had been in the Cold Stream Guards and served in the Italian campaign.

Eric laughed and asked me, "Do you know why Broadbent joined the guards?"

"That is an easy one. Roy was always a mad bugger for fine clothes. Someone told him the guards looked the most dashing in the forces, and Bob's your uncle, he went and joined them."

"Oh hush, you two," said Dorothy. "Enough about that bloody war. It's over, thank God, and there are more important things to talk about than those horrible days."

"You know Roy is back in Halifax," said Eric

"He has a foreign bride, just like you, Harry," Dorothy added in an excited voice.

"I know," I said. "He wrote me while I was in Germany and told me that he had wed a woman from Naples."

Dorothy said, "Her name is Irma, and she is really a lovely girl. I was just telling Friede that I am sure those two will become fast friends."

"Where are they now?" I asked.

"They are staying with his mother," Dorothy replied. "But you know his mum. She is such a sport, and Roy can do no wrong by her because he is her only child."

"Where are you and Friede living?"

I sighed and told her that I was back with my family until we could find suitable rooms.

Eric screamed out, "Crikey, you're living with your Ma on Boothtown Road?! Now that's showing your wife a real cockeyed view of England."

"I know," I said, ashamed.

"Luv," said Eric, speaking directly to Friede, "you might have thought us English are all mad buggers. Well, take it from me, we are, but Harry's old mum is as barmy as you can get. She is a first-rate Christmas cracker."

"Eric, please," I said, "this is serious."

"Sure thing," he said apologetically.

Dorothy was quiet for a moment and exclaimed, "I think I have the perfect idea. Why don't you move in with me?"

"What about your husband?" I asked.

Eric started to whistle as if a shell were crashing into enemy held territory.

Afterwards, Dorothy cleared her throat and said, "He did a runner."

"He did what?" I asked.

"It was a war-time marriage. You know the blitz, Dunkirk and we'll meet again, don't know where, don't know when. You know that bunch of cobblers. When he was in the forces, our marriage was great, but after peace was declared, it was like he had shellshock. He couldn't get use to tea at five and slippers on at nine, so he buggered off to Pontefract."

"Stupid Sod," I said.

Dorothy agreed and replied, "I don't think the lazy bugger is coming back anytime soon. It would be such a great help if you two came and let one of my rooms because the rent is rather dear for one person."

It was apparent to me that having lunch with those two was the best spot of luck I'd had in months. Eric even asked me as we were finishing our meal what I was doing for work. I lied and said I had a few nibbles but nothing definite.

"Once you've moved into Dorothy's house, come down and visit me at the metal works. I am in good with the boss, so he is sure to give you some work."

"I am not sure about that," I replied to Eric. "Unlike you, I've had no training working a lathe."

"There's nothing to it," said Eric. "All ya got to do is let the tool guide you and it grinds itself. Keep your thoughts free, and you are on easy street by the end of the work day."

I said, "Alright, I'll try it." I looked over at Friede and whispered, "See, everything is right as rain." She still looked a little unconvinced, but it was hard for her to observe the banter and the gossip from a world as foreign to her as her life in Hamburg was to me.

Eric added in a cautionary tone, "I can borrow my friend's Morton motor on Saturday."

"Why?" I asked.

"You are going to need it for a quick getaway from your ma. Knowing her, she'll turn into a surly old fox once she gets it between her teeth that you are flying from the happy nest."

"There'll be an even greater row," said Dorothy with a laugh, "when she finds out Eric had something to do with it. She hasn't forgiven him yet for being chased by the coppers and trying to hide in her coal shute."

"Believe you me," he said, "I rue the day she found me in the cellar instead of the coppers. What a bawling out she gave me."

When it came to my mother and money, Eric and Dorothy were not far off the mark in their assessment of her. In the Depression, she managed a few doss houses and had no remorse chucking grown men out on their ear to live on the street for being late with their rent. Necessity had turned whatever gentleness she had into a malignant tumour of remorse, regret, shame, and anger. The winding course my mother's life took from coal miner's daughter to coal miner's wife to fallen woman and finally to some crude respectability in the underclass ensured that she did not take kindly to losing a shilling.

I looked over at Friede and said, "My friends are right; we must not say anything to my mum until we are ready to leave her house."

Friede looked unsettled by this suggestion.

"Are you alright with this?" I asked.

Friede shook her head and said in German, "I don't feel comfortable doing that to your mother."

I said, "It is really for the best because she is liable to throw me out by the scruff of my collar if she thinks she is going to be short a couple of farthings."

Friede looked pained and said in a weary tone, "I really don't understand this world that you live in, here in England."

"Neither do I, but once we are at Dorothy's, everything will be better."

When we returned home that day, I kept out of my mother's way and avoided conversing with my brothers. Even though I had little money, on that Friday we took our meals outside, which pleased my mother no end.

"Saves on the washing up," she said but added cannily, "wot king's ransom are yer hiding from yer Ma that you can go out on the town and feast like a Rothschild?"

"It was just rock and chips, mam, not a night out at the Savoy. Besides," I said, "I got a job."

"Go on," responded my mother. "And thy work, is at Grosvenor's grocery?"

"No, I am starting a job at a metal works factory."

My mother laughed and said, "Mind you, don't cut thy fingers off because you were always a clumsy bugger when a lad."

In the early morning hours on the day of our liberation from my mother's house, I prayed that Eric was going to be on time. A little later on, I went downstairs to see if my mother's mood might cause our departure to turn into violent calamity.

My mother, like the giant in Jack in The Bean Stalk, and eyed my actions suspiciously.

"What has thee planned for today?"

90

"We are going out," I said evasively.

"Oh ay, another stroll around Ackroyd Park like you're to the manor born?" she said sarcastically.

"Not exactly," I responded, but by this point my mother had grown bored with chiding me. She now turned her attention towards my youngest half-brother, Bill, who had eaten bacon off his father's breakfast plate. "They'll be hell to pay when thy father gets out of the thunder box," she warned Bill. "He'll box your ear for the dog's breakfast you left him."

My youngest brother laughed with a nervous deviance while my other half-brother Matt prepared to leave the house for work. It pained me that I couldn't tell him of my plans to move from Boothtown Road, but I was afraid that he would betray my confidence. Matt was too much under my mother's shadow to trust him to keep a secret from her, especially if he was pushed or vexed at someone.

Afterwards, I rushed upstairs to our attic room, where I found Friede sitting nervously on our perfectly made bed. "It is time," I said, and we began to gather up and pack our belongings. We then waited for Eric to drive us away from my mother's confused bondage of greed, guilt, and want.

It seemed to takes ages for my friend to appear with his Morton. Time passed for us like water dripping from a leaf onto the forest floor. I became agitated by how slow everything seemed to be moving, and I lit a cigarette, which made Friede gasp for air. I paced and looked at my watch as it moved from half-past eight to quarter-two, and then five minutes to nine.

"Any minute now," I said. "It won't be long, and Eric will be here."

Friede looked nervous, and she asked me, "Is this subterfuge really necessary? Can't we just explain to your mother that we are moving?"

"No." I said in a whisper. "This is the only way. Remember when Eric comes to the door to go out and don't look back; just climb into the motor and wait for us there." I hugged her and said, "This will soon be just a funny story we can tell ourselves."

Just before nine, I heard a rap at our door.

My mother screamed out, "Would someone get the bleeding door? I am not in service, you know."

"Right, this is it," I said to Friede, and I began to instruct her. "Walk in front of me, and don't worry; I will be behind you with our luggage."

Friede put on her coat on and slung her purse over her shoulder. We both walked together from the room, and then I closed the door behind us. We came down the creaking staircase with as light a footstep as possible. By the time we reached the landing, my mother was staring at us with a vague gleam in her eyes. She was not able to comprehend why I was loaded up like a porter at a railway terminal. My mother had a puzzled look on her face as if she was trying to calculate through long sum division a reason for the baggage.

Friede froze when she got to where my mother was standing. She fumbled for a word or phrase in English or German that could express her feelings at the moment, but she could find none.

My mother blurted out, "What you've got to say to me, lass?"

Friede resigned herself to the fact that there was no word that would make my mother understand our leaving. Instead of speaking, she kissed my mother's cheek and withdrew from my mother's side.

"What's that for?" my mother said, dumbfounded.

Friede stopped, but by this time she had found some words and cast them at her. "Thank you for your kindness." With that, she opened the front door and proceeded to the waiting motor.

My mother looked out and recognized Eric standing on the front step and hissed at him, "You," as if he was a mad dog that she wanted to put down.

By this point, my mother was in complete confusion as to what was going on. She made several wide guesses as if she were playing a parlour game and settled on the most cynical explanation for the morning's turmoil: she believed Friede was leaving me. My mother gave me a wicked grin of triumph and said, "I told you she wouldn't last, lad. So it is back to Hitler land for her? You'll be better off without a Nazi. She'd be like a bleeding millstone around your neck."

Holding tightly onto our bags, I stepped around my mother and faced her from the outside of the house. I looked at her with rage, disappointment, and unwarranted disgust. I measured her trespasses against me and my sister during our country's dark and hungry years.

"Mam, you demand a credo you do not deserve, to honour thy mother." She was about to respond when I interrupted her. "Shush," I said. "You really are a stupid old bitch to think that she is leaving me. The only person being left is you."

"Wot?" she asked.

"You can keep the four days extra rent," I said, "but we have taken rooms with Dorothy Butterworth."

"You're no bloody different than anyone else," my mother said to me. "Go on, bugger off. Not one of you can stick by your mother. Ingrate!" she cried out at me.

"Too much water filled with shit has passed under our bridge, mam, for you to call me ungrateful," I retorted.

"Bloody bastard!" she screamed at me "I kept you safe. I fed you when I should have given you up to the work house. I would have been better off never marrying your father and having his three wretches. Each of you has gone and deserted thy mother. Let that be a curse upon your head, boy!"

I laughed at her and said the only curse upon me was having a mother like her.

"Do you think you could ever smarten up and just show a bit of love to your kids? It is not asking much to ask why you couldn't make any of your children feel like they were needed for something more than their wages. It wasn't my fault you married my dad, it wasn't my fault that you thought he was the answer to your prayers and found out he had more dreams than sense or that he was too old to keep a family fed in a world turned upside down."

My mother looked at me with her mouth agape, her face drained of blood and anger or the will to fight me. We stood facing each other, silent. We were no longer mother or son, but appellant and defendant in the court of family recrimination, where we were both guilty of the sin of survival.

As I watched my words dry in my mother's brain, I was at first elated, then a sickness churned in my stomach that was as strong and as deadly as typhus. It was hatred, it was shame, it was disgust, and I couldn't figure out if it was directed towards my mother or pointed at me.

My mother seemed to be infected by the same malady, and she said wearily, "Then you best go and don't look back because there is

93

now there for you anymore. Not home, not hearth, and not kin. I am as cold to you now as if I were dead. And you are now as cold to me as your poor dead sister Marion, who rots with the rest of Barnsley's poor, far from God's good grace."

Chapter Twelve:
A Postal Address beyond the Power of Man

Dorothy Butterworth's terraced one up, one down was situated just north of Gibbet Street. She and her husband had let it at the beginning of the war. They presumed that the conflict against Hitler and their tenancy in a dodgy part of town were to be brief. It came as a complete surprise to Dorothy that both the war and her occupancy lasted longer than she had expected. What also came as a surprise to Dorothy was that she had become a casualty of the war and not her husband; he had wounded her pride and damaged her faith in marriage because during the conflict he had been unfaithful.

His philandering began the moment he was issued an army tunic and realized that death was not an abstract concept, but a real possibility for him. At that point, he calculated that nothing really mattered but squeezing as much out of life as was possible during a war. He shed his wedding ring and took up smoking because, as far he was concerned, it didn't look like he or many other men were going to survive to their twenty-first birthday. Despite the bullets, the shags, and the fags, he emerged from his part in the war more or less intact.

Dorothy Butterworth's husband returned home to Halifax after the war. He seemed to her to be his old self, except for his cravings for Lucky Strikes and pretty ladies other than his wife. So, for a couple years, he passed his spare time by smoking and having meaningless trysts with shop girls, factory girls, and girls on the bus to Bradford. It seemed like nothing was going to change his pattern of unfaithfulness because his wife provided him all the comforts of home, while his girlfriends gave him what he thought he was missing and deserved.

However, it wasn't enough and one morning over toast and jam, he said, "Sorry, but being married to you just isn't my cup of tea." With that, he pushed his chair from the kitchen table, grabbed his coat, and just as he was about to walk out of the door, he told his wife, "Hope there's no hard feelings, but can't be buggering around when it all be broken." With that, he was out of her life without even a 'thank you very much.'

No matter how much Dorothy's husband legging it was a domestic tragedy for them, for me it was a stroke of luck. The only drawback to this new living arrangement was that Dorothy's home was not in the most desirable location. The street Dorothy lived on had never seen better days, and I doubted that it ever would unless it was demolished. During daylight hours, the road was cast in a sinister grey pallor because it was enclosed on three sides by a series of industrial buildings that joined together and formed a menacing wall around the neighbourhood. At night time, it felt even more oppressive in the enclosure because there were only a few outdoor gas lights.

Down at the residents' local, many said as a joke that "it was to keep the riff raff out," whereas others believed that the wall marked the enclosure of a ghetto, possibly built centuries ago to house religious undesirables. The true reason for the wall didn't really matter because everyone in the area knew that fortune rarely favoured those that lived on the wrong side of that brick fortification.

Eric couldn't hide his dismay when we arrived at Dorothy's worker's terrace. Grinning, he remarked while scanning the derelict conditions of the street, "Crickey, I'll keep the motor running because I don't trust the natives." He became mesmerised by the wall that loomed across the back of the houses on the other side of the street and said, "Bloody hell, it looks like you're in a gaol. Are you going to have to tunnel to get out of here?" he said sarcastically.

"Pretty much," I said dejectedly, "or use the ginnel we came through to get onto the street."

"This place has gone to complete buggery," said Eric with good humour.

"It's not as bad as that," I responded defensively. "At least," I said, "they weren't daft when they put in that ginnel because at the other end of that tunnel are two shops on either side of the entrance that keep everyone that lives here in the right frame of mind."

"Oh aye," he said. "I bet one's a boozer and the other a butcher's shop."

"Too right," I replied. "The off license does a brisk trade in beer and harsh spirits. I don't think I'll be too keen on the butcher because it seems he does more business in offal, kidney, or tripe rather than a Barnsley chop."

"You seem to know an awful lot about this new neighbourhood," said Eric, "considering you just arrived today. Did you date a bird on this road before the war?"

"No," I laughed and replied, "yesterday while Friede was resting, I decided to reconnoitre our new digs. I wanted to get a feel for the area."

"Anything else to report?" he asked and helped Friede lift her bags from the motor.

"Nothing really, except that I wouldn't want to be a mouse in these parts."

"Oh? Why?" he asked.

I explained that on my explorations, I had discovered that an army of feral cats patrolled the opening of the ginnel as if they were spawns of Cerberus. Judging from the smell inside the walkway, the felines were using it as if it were a urinal inside a workman's club.

"The moggies are very combative," I said. "If you ever come on foot, watch out for those blighters because they will set upon your legs like a pack of cheetahs going after a lame zebra."

Eric chuckled, and Friede joined in with our amusement. She suddenly stopped laughing and began to cough furiously.

"Are you alright?" I asked.

"Yes, I am fine. It is just that the air...it is horrible...it is so thick with rubbish."

I took from my pocket a clean handkerchief and gave it to Friede. She thanked me and used it to cover her face because a breeze had picked up and brought our way a cloud of dust and coal soot. It floated around us like it was the building block for a new galaxy on the edge of the Milky Way.

When the gusts finally died down, Eric offered us cigarettes from a silver case. "Let's have a fag break before we finish the job."

I took two cigarettes, lit them, and passed one onto Friede.

"Thanks," Friede said as she inhaled a good brand of tobacco.

She looked up at the sky, which was overcast, and asked, "Does this city ever get any sun?"

"It is in your ration book," said Eric. "You are allowed two portions per month. And if you skive from anyone else's, they will throw you in the nick."

We both laughed, and then grew quiet as a couple old women walked passed us. They were hunched over like Pharaoh's Israelite slaves. They could even have been hunchbacks from the Middle Ages, off to bell ringing class.

Eric stopped his joking and said, "Pitiful isn't it? What all those old gals needed from the state when they were kids was a bit of bloody milk."

"Bloody rickets," I muttered. "You know whose fault that is?" I asked rhetorically. "It's the fault of the bloody Tories," I said in disgust at the crippling but preventable affliction.

"At least now," Eric replied, "the nippers get a milk ration to stop Britain being known as the isle of hunchbacks."

I tossed my cigarette onto the ground and looked around my new neighbourhood. I could feel a wave of disgust rising from within the pit of my stomach.

"What are you thinking?" Eric asked me.

"Nothing much," I said so as not to worry Friede. I smiled towards her and said, "I was thinking it will be nice to get a cup of tea."

A cuppa was the farthest thing from my mind at that moment. In fact, I was agitated by each new occurrence that I witnessed on the road. It made me feel both anger and embarrassment that we had to move into this area. I hoped that our taking up residence here was not the first step in a downward spiral to a permanent life in a garret.

At that moment, some children walked by us and argued about the merits of some footballer in loud, gruff voices. They sounded older and braver than their years. It was as if they weren't afraid of anything except perhaps their future. They wore scruffy corduroy trousers, thin worker's jackets, and woollen caps that rode jauntily on top of their heads. On the pavement, one of the youths spotted my partially smoked cigarette and scooped it up. He cheekily called over to my direction and said, "Ta."

Miserable buggers, I thought and grew depressed as I watched them disappear from sight.

"Nothing has changed," I said to Eric sadly. "Those bairns don't look any better off than we did at that age. Didn't we fight a war for something?" I asked.

"Sure we did, but Harry, it wasn't for those poor sods."

"Too right," I said wearily. "You know what Malthus said about uz folk and those kids who just walked down the lane?"

"Malthus who?" asked Eric. "Is he a mate of yours?"

"Don't be daft," I said. "He wrote books in the last century that are now used to justify inequality, poor housing, and hopelessness."

"Oh," said, Eric, "and there I thought you were going to tell me a joke. Better go on then and hop on your hobby horse and tell me about this bloke."

I ignored his chiding and said, "The bloke, as you so eloquently call him, wrote hundreds of pamphlets about the scourge of poverty corrupting the nation at the time. He deduced there was no way out of it and stated that *To prevent the recurrence of misery is, alas! Beyond the power of man.'* After he published that, every churchman, businessman, and lord in the realm felt that they could sleep soundly at night because the cursed lives of many Britons were caused by God, and man held no blame. So there is nothing," I said with growing anger, "going to change the fate of the weak, the poor, and the sick in this land because we are always finding ways to justify it. The hopeless in England are as close to Heaven as an amoebae floating in the calm Sargasso Sea."

"I guess you did learn something in them books at the library when you should have been chasing girls at the park, like me and Roy," Eric said, trying to lighten my gloom.

Friede interrupted me and said, "I am sure it is nice to talk politics, but shouldn't we get a move on? Can't we get our bags into the house and start our life together?"

"Yes, you're right. I am sorry for talking Eric's ear off. He should get on with his day, and so should we."

Friede grabbed my hand and said with trepidation, "Well, come on. Let's see what is in store for us in our new flat."

As we started to move up towards the house, Dorothy opened up her door and came outside to meet us.

"Looks like that's my cue to be on my way," said Eric.

He kissed Friede, patted me on the shoulder, and waved hello and goodbye to Dorothy. He made a quick joke to all of us and jumped into his motor and disappeared.

When Dorothy met us at the door stoop, she looked at Friede and saw that she was in turmoil. Friede looked like a salt water fish trying to survive in a cold water canal.

"Come here, luv, it's not as bad as all that," she said, "'cause after the rain comes the sunshine in our Halifax. I know around here it looks a bit rough and ready for a good scrub. But it won't take long for you to take a shine to our street." Pointing to her heart, she said, "Remember, luv, in Halifax, it's what's on the inside that counts because on the outside it all looks like a busman's bollocks. Isn't that the truth?" Dorothy said to me, giving me a conspiratorial wink.

"I wouldn't go that far," I responded, "but Friede will get the hang of the place sooner than you can say Jack Robinson."

Dorothy gave Friede a friendly hug and said, "You've got a good man in our Harry, and I know you had a right ordeal with his mum. But don't fret because you are safe from that dragon in your new home. I also know something about our Harry. He's like a cat and always lands feet first. I'd give my right hand to have a bloke like Harry as my husband rather than the blighter who wed me."

Friede walked towards me and touched my hand in reassurance. I didn't know what to say to her and instead tried to calm both our fears by whispering, "Today, we must make do, but it won't be long and we will be away from here, and in much better circumstances. Everyone in England is in the same leaky boat because the ruddy war bled us dry. Our time will come soon."

Friede looked relieved and said, "I am sure it will be alright. I have to see it as an adventure and that whatever danger comes our way, we will end up safe on the right side of the river bank."

"That's it," I said, "treat all of this like it was part of a jolly good yarn, and we'll be able to laugh about this rough patch in the years to come."

At that moment, I had a hard time in believing that any laughter was going to come from this. I was starting to doubt whether I could pull it off and make a go of it in post-war Yorkshire. I started to fear that my marriage was about to capsize and that I would drown alone and unloved.

There was something else that terrified me, and it was something that I had kept well hidden from Friede. It was that there were more streets like this across the British Isles than proper ones. It was how

Britain had always done its business with its citizens. *Give 'em nowt but lash, or they will demand the keys to the kingdom.* "If things get too bad," I said to myself, "I will let her go like a bird to return to the safety of her family in Germany."

I resolved that Friede was not going to be ruined by this country like my dad, my mom, and my sister. I wouldn't let that happen to her. No, I made myself promise that day that I would rather lose her than see her sink into the nameless, soul crushing, industrialized destitution that England offered most of its citizens.

When we walked inside of Dorothy's house, I was overcome with claustrophobia because it felt no bigger than a telephone box. The lower floor consisted of a narrow front entrance, which led off to a small parlour, a staircase, and a scullery at the back.

Dorothy ushered us into the sitting room and uttered the phrase, "Cheap but cheerful."

Inside, there was a settee with a brightly coloured blanket thrown over it to hide its antiquity. On the outer wall was a diminutive fire place, which was the only source of heat in the home. Dorothy pointed to the empty grate and said, "You two will do just fine by cuddling to stay warm. I'm going to need a pullover at night."

At the far end of the room, two wooden chairs were placed around a table that held a box with electrical wires going into the wall.

"What's that?" I asked.

Dorothy laughed and said, "That is Yorkshire ingenuity. It's a wireless box and the cheapest way of getting music into your house next to buying a ukulele.

"I have never seen anything like it before in my life," I said, dumbfounded.

My friend explained that there was a radio shop on Gibbet Street that sold subscriptions for area residents who didn't have the money to buy their own wireless.

"It's only twenty-five pence a week," Dorothy stated.

"I still don't understand how it works," I said.

It was then Dorothy pointed to a wire that ran down the wall and was connected to the back of the box. She explained that the radio shop had strung it up from their receiver and across the rooftops on her street. A workman then drilled a hole in each rooftop and dropped a connecting cable into the parlours of the homes below. Each subscriber received an amplifier that was encased in cheap wood. Its volume and reception were sketchy at the best of times, and it only broadcasted whatever frequency was set on the receiver back at the radio shop.

"Sometimes it plays decent dance music, but most of the time it's just ruddy static," Dorothy said, pointing to the inert box.

Friede walked over to it and stroked the amplifier's mesh grill as if it were a family pet and addressed Dorothy wistfully, "When I lived in Germany, I loved to dance."

Dorothy laughed and said, "Well, Harry, you have your work cut out for you if you are going to have to take two of Halifax's most glamorous girls out on the town for a night of dancing. I hope you finally learned how to shake a leg while you were away in the RAF"

I said with bravado, "I know a thing or two about dancing." Both women looked at each other and then back at me, whereupon they fell into giggles at my alleged mastery of dancing.

Afterwards, Dorothy showed us the kitchen, which was much smaller than the sitting room. For cooking, there was a geriatric gas oven with a two-ring hob. At the far end of the short kitchen stood a dilapidated side board that contained a slim assortment of plates and cups. On the outside wall below the window was a shallow stone sink. A large hook-shaped tap jutted out from it and provided cold briny water like a miser produces five pound notes. To the side of it, a tin bath rested on the cold rock floor.

Dorothy pointed to it and said to Friede, "Sorry, it is not the most comfortable way to have a bath."

"That's alright," said Friede and tapped the sheet metal with one of her fingers.

"It takes ages for the kettle to fill the tub with hot water. Taking a bath here is about as enjoyable as washing up in the North Sea on New Year's Day. It's probably better to use the local council baths, which are about a mile away."

The Spartan room also contained a kitchen table. Its surface was chipped and scratched, and one of its legs was game, which made it wobble like a sickly spinster on her way to church.

In the narrow hallway, a rail thin staircase led to a small upper floor bedroom. At the top of the landing beside the single room was another door. Behind it were concealed steps, which climbed up to the attic that had been turned it into a spare room by Dorothy's husband before he bolted.

Dorothy had insisted that we take her bedroom for ourselves. "It's only right, luv, as there are two of you and only one of me. What do I need that big bed for?"

But we refused the offer. "Seeing that you got me out of a tight squeeze with my Ma, I wouldn't hear of it. We'll do just fine up in the crow's nest," I said. Besides, I didn't want to take too many liberties with Dorothy's friendship, as I really didn't know how long we were going to stay.

For tea that night, I went to a chippy and brought back a takeaway. In the kitchen, the three of us ate soggy chips and scraps of fish wrapped in a flaccid batter with little interest. Afterwards, we went to the parlour to listen to the amplifier, and I tried to relax.

I spent most of the evening smoking cigarettes and staring nervously through the parlour window onto an empty street.

"What are you looking at?" Friede asked while she sat on a settee and chatted with Dorothy.

"Nothing," I said, and Dorothy replied, "Then you better get away from it because it will turn into something."

The tubercular colour of daylight began to wane, and the parlour was draped in shadow. Dorothy looked at her watch and said while she turned on two small gas lights fixed to the wall, "You would think that the days would be getting longer by now."

At nine o'clock, we said good night to Dorothy.

Dorothy kissed both us and said, "If I were you, I'd take Friede to the loo straight away because it is a right bloody ordeal to get into once you've got sleep in your eyes."

I took a torch and led Friede outside to the toilets. Friede looked up and down the street and asked, "Is our privy at the rail station?"

"No," I said dismissively. "We must walk to the end of the row of houses, where there will be a back alley, and the bog will be there."

Friede followed me, and I could feel her angry breath behind me. "Mind yourself," I said to Friede and cast the beam of light ahead of us.

"Where to now?" Friede asked.

I said, "I think it is right here," and swung my torch until I saw a series of interconnected cement bogs that had a corresponding house number on them.

Friede cursed in German, "Thunder and lightning."

I tried to make light of the primitive toilets by saying, "For an outdoor privy, they are rather posh because they come with a lock and key. As a lad, I'd be lucky if the WC had a door, let alone a key."

I stuck the key into the lock and fumbled around until the wooden door swung open. I handed Friede the torch, clicked my heels like a German railway ticket collector, and said, "Madam, for your comfort, inside this luxurious commode is a copy of the Daily Mail. It has been torn into strips by your trusty servants to provide you an enjoyable time in Halifax's best bog."

Before I closed the door behind her, she bowed to me and giggled.

I lit a cigarette while Friede spoke from the toilet and said they had better toilets on the farm she was evacuated to in Coburg during the war.

"Perhaps," I said, "but you never had anyone as gallant waiting for you outside." With that, I heard her laugh, and she opened up the door. She saw my cigarette and asked for a puff.

"I am sorry, Harry, but I am finding it hard to get adjusted to England. How does anyone ever get used to their homes and neighbourhoods if they all look like this?"

"I don't think anyone ever gets comfortable if they have to live like this," I said. "But for us, we are just visiting, and we'll find a better place soon." I hoped the promise of new lodgings would allay her growing disappointment with me and this new world she was forced to inhabit.

Friede sucked on her cigarette, and after some deliberation said, "I will have to find something to do, a job, anything, or else I will go mad," while we walked back towards the house.

When I came inside, Dorothy reminded us to light some candles. "The gas light only goes as far as the first floor."

We climbed to our upstairs bedroom, and both of us carried a candle that was tightly wedged into brass holders. "At least here," I said, "we get two candles, unlike at my mother's place."

104

The flames flickered and cast long shadows against the walls as we made our way to our room in the attic.

Friede undressed behind a mobile screen and put on a night dress that she had brought with her from Germany. She tiptoed over the cold floor while holding onto the billowing candle. Friede cast a silhouette against the attic's slopping wall, which made her look like an apparition. As soon as she got into bed, she gutted her light and buried herself under the bed covers. "Sorry," she said in a sleepy tone, "but I can speak no more; I am dead tired." She then waved goodnight to me.

I removed my clothes with less haste than Friede and folded them neatly onto a chair. I got into a pair of pyjamas and slipped into bed. As soon as Friede noticed that I was beside her, she turned her back to me and fell quickly into a distraught sleep. I lay awake for some time and listened to her shallow, dream-filled breathing. Underneath our heavy blankets, I felt her limbs tremble, but I wasn't sure if it was caused by a cold draft blowing through the tiny cracks in the wall or her growing emotional exhaustion.

Chapter Thirteen:
The Queue for spring

Sundays in Halifax were as somnolent as a holy shrine at sundown. Everything was shuttered and bolted down tight, from shops to cinemas to emotions. The only institutes open were the churches, and I wasn't keen on spending my day off listening to the warbling of alcoholic and sinful men of the cloth tell me how to be a better Christian or man. Anyways, my guilt wasn't something that could be washed away with rosary beads and a couple Hail Marys; it was only going to go away when my life turned 'round.

One thing was for certain: it didn't happen during our first Sunday at Dorothy's because I was exhausted and Friede was worn to a dull flint. We were listless except when it came to being irritable and easily wounded. By the end of breakfast, we stopped trying to say anything to each other because every word spoken became sharper and shriller than the next. When afternoon dragged itself around, we listened tensely to the wireless box until the static became too much to endure.

In the end, we abandoned any hope of doing anything special that day; instead, we retreated up to our musky room, where I felt anxious and trapped in its small space. Behind the closed door of our sleeping den, I started to smoke incessantly, and Friede remarked, "Must you destroy what little fresh air we have?"

"Sorry," I said and stubbed out the cigarette and started to whistle an irritating tune, which made Friede even more ill-tempered. "Instead of making music, maybe you can come up with some preparations for the coming weeks. What are we going to do for work?" she asked plaintively.

"I do have a plan," I said defensively.

"Well then, I wish you would share it with me so that I know we are going to be alright," she said.

I tried to touch Friede's arm, but she bristled at my closeness and shooed me away. In the end, we escaped each other by finding a book to read, and for the rest of the day, apart from our rhythmic breathing; our world was quiet, apart from an alarm clock that ticked away until afternoon turned to evening.

The following day, Eric swung around to our house and told me that he had made good on his promise. "I spoke about you to the boss man, and he expects you to come see him tomorrow about a job."

I thanked him, and the following morning I arrived at the metal works factory for my interview. The establishment wasn't as impressive as Eric had described it. I was expecting to see a bustling enterprise about the size of an Avro engine assembly plant; instead, it was a non- descript industrial building that was situated near the city's football pitch.

Eric may have embellished the grandeur of his workplace surroundings, but to his credit, he bestowed the same type of polish on my qualification, and that convinced his employer to consider me for service. "Sure, he can do the work because he learns quickly. Once my mate Harry gets the hang of a machine, watch out because he is like a great musician playing an instrument."

The owner was around seventy with bushy white hair and big horn rimmed glasses, and he looked like a village blacksmith. Overtop of his workman overalls, he wore a heavy leather smock that ran from the top of his chest to just above his knees. He pounded it like a gorilla and then shouted, "These are the vestments for an honest day's labour, lad."

He proudly explained to me that from the moment the shop opened in the 1930s, he'd always worked right alongside his team because "a bit of elbow grease gets the job done, if you get my meaning, son?"

I was about to tell him that hard work didn't scare me because I'd been doing it since I was able to walk, but the owner interrupted me. "Beg yer pardon," he screamed and cupped a giant hand covered in dirt to his ear. "I am a bit deaf because of the machines, so speak up."

I yelled back in an assertive tone, realizing that he couldn't hear my words but was able to register the timber of my voice, "I can only do my best, but I don't know my arse from my elbow when it comes to making tools."

The owner seemed satisfied by my pantomime, and he ended our interview by shaking my hand. He yelled into my ear as if I were also hard of hearing, "During the war, you served your country, so I think

108

you can serve me in peace time. I know you won't muck about. Work begins at half-seven, and ends at four. Don't be late."

When I came home that day, Friede asked me how my interview went. "I got it," I said and added, "we won't have to fish into our savings anymore." A look of relief washed across Friede's face. "That is wonderful," she said and kissed my cheek.

I smiled and decided that it wasn't worth my while to tell her that I was on sufferance and that I was only being paid an apprentice's wages. Still, I knew it was something to be earning money again, despite the amount. The machine shop, I reasoned, was a start, but I seriously doubted my career path would last long in precision tool making.

Even if being a skilled workman had been my passion, it didn't take the foreman long to spot my ignorance and ineptitude at running a lathe. He wasn't going to abide my inadequacies, and he put me on notice that my employment was in jeopardy if I didn't wise up.

"All thumbs are we, Smith?" queried the foreman as he came over to my work station and looked at my handiwork. "Well, well," he said while he binned a tool I had ground down into a useless mess. "I can see you would have been a right bloody joker to have in shop during the war. Lad, it wasn't that long ago, but maybe you remember when it were on?"

"Kettle?" I asked sarcastically.

"Don't be daft with me, Lad. I'm talking about the war, when we were all in it together. In those days," he said, speaking as if he were an expert on total warfare, "we made first-grade spanners, hammers, and the like for the RAF and the Royal Navy. You could say," he said, filled with unwarranted self-importance, "our contribution made a difference in how the war turned out. You could even say that without our first-rate men slaving away at their lathes, many a serviceman would be dead and buried, if not for the top job tools we made during the war."

"I am sure you could say that," I said, wiping the grease from my fingers with a filthy cloth.

The foreman shook his head in contempt at me and blurted out angrily, "Someone like you shouldn't forget that," he said while eyeing me with contempt.

"And maybe the chaps using them played a small part in the victory," I interjected.

"Shut it," the foreman said to me and shook his finger at me. "I am not going to have us lose the peace with this rubbish," he said. "Can't have a man in shop that's got no feel for the lathe; it's like hiring a one-legged man to teach roller skating."

I looked at him, infuriated by his smug arrogance, which was as corpulent as his waistline. Flippantly, I replied, "I can tell you what I didn't do in the war. I didn't get a cushy selective service job."

The foreman snorted about like an animal in a paddock, then after much deliberation he finally said, "Don't tempt me, Smith, because I'll have you out on your ear today if that is what you want. Do you?" he asked provocatively.

"Not particularly," I answered and picked up my protective goggles and put them back on over my eyes. I turned from him and turned a knob that started my lathe rotating and returned to my duties to silence the foreman's hectoring.

On one of our cigarette breaks, Eric told me that he had seen the altercation between me and the foreman. My mate looked worried and said, "Mind yourself with him, Harry; he is a proper bastard."

"Bugger him," I responded. "I really appreciate that you got me this job. You are a first-class mate, but I don't think I will be sticking around much longer if I have to deal with that mad git. I guess I am not cut out to make tools," I said. "Anyways, all around town, there are plenty of jobs for the asking. I don't want to get stuck here with someone busting my chops, especially when I can find another that might give me a chance for a better future."

Eric looked at me and agreed with what I had said. He told me that if I left, he had no hard feelings. "Just helping out a mate, and besides, if you stay much longer, you'll bankrupt the whole bleeding company with all of the shoddy spanners you are making."

At the end of the work day, an elderly secretary who doubled as the paymaster came by to give each employee their weekly wages. I opened my envelope and discovered it had more silver than notes, but that was alright because I knew I wasn't going to be staying there long. *I'll find another job before anyone tries to sack me*, I thought.

I walked out of the shop and felt elated that it was Friday because I had two whole days to spend with Friede. Above me, however, a thick pattern of clouds hovered and looked malignant with rain. I had no umbrella and no inclination to walk home and be drowned on the way like a rat. So I hopped onto a double- decker bus that was heading towards Gibbet Street.

When I handed the conductor my fare, he punched out my ticket with his portable device. "Ta," I said, and he grinned back at me and said something quick and funny about the rain outside.

The bus resumed its route, and I climbed upstairs to have a cigarette. While up top, I gazed out from bus' large window and witnessed a spring rain restlessly settle across Halifax. The storm was intense, and I surmised that it must have come from a gale blown in from the English Channel.

By the time my bus passed Saville Road the rain had tired of causing mayhem, and was now just drizzle that spattered against the window. A tired looking woman with bow legs and a mesh shopping bag filled with soaked groceries came up the stairs and sat beside me. She sparked up a half-finished cigarette and whispered to me, "Gawd that taste good." I smiled and turned my eyes back towards the world outside of the window. It was now just after five p.m., and the mills had let out. It was like a sluice gate had opened up to allow Atlantic Salmon to spawn to the rivers of their birth. Everywhere I looked, I saw mill women fighting their way home to prepare their families' evening tea.

Through the rain, I observed their water-stained images. Every one of them had their umbrellas deployed, and beneath each black dome the females looked identical. All wore around their heads faded kerchiefs that hid their hair while long pale rain coats obscured the contour of their bodies, as if they were nuns from a strict order.

The woman beside me began to cough, and then she spat into a handkerchief and whispered, "Ope I'm not be coming down with something."

I grunted something that didn't sound very polite and returned to looking at the unhappiness outside of my window rather than what was sitting right beside me. When my bus finally reached the Odeon theatre, I jumped off and joined the pedestrian pilgrimage towards home. Down Commercial Street, I darted and skirted between the packs of women, whose lips were pinched in worry and whose faces were as white as urinal enamel.

111

I could almost hear their silent anxiety. It was like a long burst of Morse code that always telegraphed the same message to me: *Why did I get this fried bread and drippings life instead of a better one? No sense complaining; it could be worse. My husband could be lame or I could have the cancer. Got to get a move on, or else the evening tea will be late.*

As I got closer to home, I decided to duck into a grocer's shop and pick up something for our Saturday lunch. When I swung open the glass door, a metal bell tinkled above it, but its noise was muted because inside the shop was a crowd of disgruntled customers. I stamped my feet dry and was overcome by a wet and woollen odour emanating from water logged coats, hats, and scarves.

"Crikey," I whispered and thought perhaps this wasn't the best of ideas. At that moment, a discordant symphony of people coughing, clearing their throats, or scuffing their shoes against the cement floor began to beat a tune. It was a melody I knew well; it was a song of impatience and frustration at knowing that even when you got to the front of line, there was nothing decent to buy.

Someone who was fed up with their place in the queue spat out, "Not for love or bloody money can you get a decent piece of roast beef in this country."

A buxom woman who wore cats' eyes glasses with impenetrable thick lenses added to the general mood of dissatisfaction by saying, "We must have shipped it all off to the bloody French and Germans."

"Don't forget the Wogs and Poles," someone shouted.

"Hard to forget them 'cause they live ere now, the dirty buggers," answered the woman with thick glasses.

Now it seemed it was everyone's turn in the crowd to whinge and hiss like a bunch of cats in the pitch of night. "It's bad enough that we had to stand in shop to get a rasher of bacon when the war were on. But now it's bloody over, and we're still standing around waiting to get a lolly. And once you get to the front of the line, you get nowt but bugger all. I hate to see what we get if we lost the blasted war?"

"You'd be hanging in the butcher's window instead of that old scrawny chicken that they put there for display," a voice cried out from the queue. Suddenly, everyone's anger dissipated and turned into laughter.

The stopper is back on the bottle for now, I thought. Yet, I knew it wouldn't take much for it to explode again because tempers were short, especially since the lines for scarce goods grew in size every day all across Britain.

Considering that I was skint, my choices were already limited to what was abundant and cheap. I knew that all I could afford on my wages was some head cheese and a good loaf of bread, so there was nothing for me to moan about. I patiently waited my turn and played with the coins in my trouser pocket. By the time I was at the front of the counter, I started to laugh at the thought that the only thing Britain had in abundance was pig's brains in jelly.

After getting my rations, I quickly left the butcher's shop and went to an off-license to get a couple bottles of beer. I reasoned that I was probably going to get the chop on Monday; so I better enjoy myself over the weekend.

When I came outside with my beer, head cheese, and bread shoved underneath my coat, I made a hasty retreat for home. I knew that the even though the rain had abated, I doubted the reprieve was going to last long. I wasn't wrong because suddenly the wind picked up and started blowing people about like bits of loose rubbish.

Along the way, I saw people holding on to their hats or trying to get control over their unwieldy umbrellas, but it was too late. There was an explosion of thunder, and from behind I heard someone mutter, "Ere comes the water works." Then the rain fell hard, cold, and heavy and turned our city into an even more dark and dreary place than it normally was.

When I arrived home, Friede greeted me at the door and remarked, "You look a fright." She then began to laugh as I tried to stamp my feet dry on the thin mat in the hallway.

Dorothy called out from the parlour, "I bet you look a real sight for sore eyes. You should get yourself cleaned up because Friede's made us a lovely tea. And we've got company."

"Who?" I asked in a surprised tone.

"Our Roy and his Irma popped 'round for a visit," she responded warmly.

Excitedly, I rushed into the parlour to greet my boyhood friend.

"You're a real sight for sore eyes," he said in a thick Yorkshire accent, dripping with honest delight.

113

"You, too, "I said.

"Come over here; I want you to meet someone," he said. Roy then led me towards the couch, where his wife sat. He introduced me to her with, "She's my better half, by far."

Irma seemed to be as rare a breed as Friede was in Halifax. Roy's wife had an exotic beauty that made me think that she had walked straight off the pages of a movie magazine and into our dowdy flat. I noticed that she wore a very expensive dress, which had not come from any shop in this town. Around her neck, Irma wore a string of fat pearls that seemed to cast a rich reflection up towards her oval face, which was the colour of pale olives.

Roy's wife's hands were adorned with an expensive engagement and wedding band while dangerous red nail polish flared our like a tiger's paw after she had killed her prey. I watched her eyes register my presence, and they flashed an equal measure of sensuality, danger, and playfulness.

It was a complete shock for me to see my friend Roy married to a woman who was so utterly different than him. Roy was many things, but one thing he was not was adventurous. As long as I had known him, he liked one brand of beer, one brand of butter, and he was against any type of surprise.

Roy read the disbelief on my face and interjected, "After all those fireworks I went through in Italy, I am just right bloody chuffed to have ended up with their most fetching girl."

I extended my hand to Irma, which made her laugh at me. She said in a throaty Italian accent, "Your wife tells me you are wise to European customs."

"Yes, I suppose I am," I said confidently.

"Then why do you greet me like a banker on High Street?" she asked. "A handshake will never do when you are saying hello to an Italian woman."

Irma then kissed me fully on both cheeks. "Now, that has brought the blood back to your face," she said, satisfied.

"I'd say it has," I responded.

Irma then came closer up to me and said, "Dear, dear, this will never do."

"What won't?" I asked, dumbfounded.

"I have smeared my lipstick all over your face. Roy!" she screamed. "Roy!"

My friend was standing beside me, lost in reverie over his wife, when the third yell awoke him from his dreams. "Don't be such a slouch, and hand me your handkerchief so I can clean your friend's face."

"It is nothing," I said as I tried to use my hands to remove it.

"Tut, tut," she said impatiently and imperiously grabbed the handkerchief that Roy had extended to her as if he were a servant. Irma then cleaned my face as if I were an eight-year-old school boy caught playing in the mud.

"Thanks," I said and went over to Friede and kissed her hello. Afterwards, I excused myself by saying I was a dripping mess and left the room singing the Perry Como song *I'm always chasing rainbows.*

When I came back down, we all sat in the kitchen to eat a stew that Friede had created from Spam and chicken stock. Roy and Irma had brought with them a bottle of Chianti to enhance our supper.

"I took as much wine as I could when we left Italy," Irma said, "but because I have been here for a year, I don't have many left to enjoy," she said dejectedly. "But Roy promises me we will go back soon for a visit."

"Friede asked Irma what she thought about her adoptive country.

"It's difficult because the English have no warmth in their hearts. England is a cold world, and I miss Naples so much. At this time of year, the orange and lemon groves would be bursting with fruit. Italy is a land of food and love, whereas Britain is a country of customs, laws, eccentrics, and horrible coffee."

Roy interrupted his wife to tell me about his job at the McIntosh chocolate factory. "Harry," he said, "you should go down there and put your name in for a job because I promise you, it's a position for life."

Irma turned to her husband and said in a loud, irritated voice, "See, Roy is a perfect example of how crazy people are in England."

"What do you mean?" I asked. "Roy isn't crazy."

"No," said Irma, "but he is content, and that to me is insane."

"How 'em I content, luv?" asked Roy. "I'm always doing things."

Irma gave him a sour look and said, "You're as happy as a cow in the field. . If my family in Italy only knew I gave up everything to marry a man who makes chewing gum, they'd cut their throats."

"We do alright with my job at Mackintosh's," Roy said in his defence, then, "we live in a lovely home."

Irma raised her glass of wine and drank it down in one gulp, then said, "Don't talk to me about that home. It is your mother's house, and for a wife to live with a man's mother is like asking two vipers to share the same bed." Irma than began arguing to herself in Italian until her husband pacified her by saying, "I'll buy you that dress you had your eyes on in the shop on Commercial Street." Roy then went back to eating his stew.

At that point, Dorothy waxed over how savoury everything had tasted.

Friede looked pleased but said with a little hesitation, "It is not an old family recipe. It was something I learned to make from the provisions Harry brought me and my family when the hunger winter was raging across Germany."

"It was a horrible time for ordinary Germans," I remarked. The food shortages were horrendous and the people were transformed into walking skeletons. Say what you will about the cause of that blasted war and the crimes of the Nazis, but innocents in their millions on every side were sent to their slaughter."

"Amen," Friede responded and swallowed the last of her wine.

I started to clear away the plates, and Roy jumped into to help, and I said to the women to go into the sitting room. "We'll do the washing up for a change."

They left the kitchen and cooed light-heartedly at our domesticity.

For the rest of the evening, we sat near a comfortable fire in the grate and listened to the radio and played cards. On the hour of eight, the news announcer remarked about the growing tensions in Germany between the Soviets and the Allies. Friede grew quiet, and I said, trying to reassure her, "It is nothing; just politicians earning their keep and newsmen selling gossip."

Chapter Fourteen:
Friends and Expats

Spring left Halifax as it had done since I was a lad: it stormed out under heavy clouds and intermittent rain showers. The sun tried its best to stretch its light and extend the daytime hours, but its rays were lukewarm, coloured grey and pale in texture. As we inched towards the solstice, the days struggled like a marathon runner going uphill after a long race, but it proved to be an exhausting sprint towards summer.

By the end of June, my heart began to ache for the beauty of distant lands, where one was caressed by warm, lithe rays of sunshine and everything was in bloom. Every morning while I dressed for work in our drab and stagnant attic room, my mind wandered to the Tahitian life of Gauguin. *If only we could live on a tropical paradise rather than in an archipelago of want*, I mused, *and then my life would be a charmed existence.* However, by the time my suspenders were firmly attached to my shoulders, the images of the Pacific Ocean breaking carefree against a deserted beach vanished and reality drowned me with the prospect of another day.

Mornings were no easier for Friede and one day I caught her sobbing.

"What is it?" I asked.

"Oh, it is nothing," she responded as she forlornly gazed at a painting hanging on the wall opposite our bed. "The water colour makes me remember something that happened long ago," Friede said and wiped her eyes dry with the sleeve from her dress.

I started to groom my hair with the hard RAF brush they had given me at induction, and I tried to find some significance to that painting. I'd honestly paid no attention to it until Friede's outburst. All I knew about it was that her mother had given it to her as a memento to remember home.

There didn't seem to be much to it, in my opinion. In fact, it was a rather pedestrian watercolour of two vagabonds sitting on a bench. Behind them was a bucolic setting of trees and nature, while the old men in rumpled clothes gazed optimistically towards a horizon that evaporated away from the canvas.

117

Friede noticed my puzzled look and said in an impatient tone, "It is called 'The Wanderers'. A man named Otto Quante painted it. He had a solid reputation in Germany for creating these types of paintings, which were unsophisticated but very popular with the public. I suppose it was because they were apolitical and reminded everyone of a time before the Nazis. He probably painted thousands of these types of paintings. Do you know why my mother gave me this particular painting?"

"No," I said and started to tie my shoelaces.

"When I was little, my mother took me to an art exhibition in Hamburg. For the event, she wore a fabulous dress and looked like a movie star. After we had inspected many paintings, my mother asked me to do her a favour. Mutti told me she couldn't decide which painting to buy. So, she asked me to choose a picture for her. It thrilled me that my mutti had made me feel so important and special and given me such a responsible task."

"That's very nice," I said, distracted by my own memories of being eight. I didn't voice my remembrance, but at that time the only painting we owned was a giant oil portrait of my grandfather, a well-respected publican. It was one of the few things we took from one lodging house to the next, and I remembered how his giant face scowled down from his perch at our poverty and threadbare existence."

"It is a special memory for me," Friede said with more emphasis, "because I didn't get much opportunity to spend a lot of time with my mother when I was a child."

"If it were my mother you had, you'd consider that a blessing," I said sarcastically.

Friede looked at me disapprovingly and replied, "I know there is bad blood between you and your mother, but there must have been some happy moments that you can remember when you were small. Besides, you can't be angry at me or others for having their good memories. It is not like I didn't have sad experiences as well."

"I suppose you're right," I said grudgingly. "And, yes, we had some happy times, but they were rationed like butter is today. It was something you got and enjoyed for five minutes every month, and you endured the rest of the time in silent agony. I am also not saying that there weren't others that had a worse go of it than me and my

118

sister, but it was still hell for us. Best way, luv, is to bury the past in a pit or at sea and keep going, because it is dead. What matters is the now and tomorrow. The past is a country I don't want to ever visit again."

Friede had a frustrated look on her face as if I didn't comprehend her words properly. "I don't want you to be cross with me, but you must let go of all that hurt, Harry. It can't stay with you because it keeps you like a man in chains. It will imprison your spirit and all of your possibilities."

"How do you know that?" I asked defensively.

"Because I feel that my past has started to imprison me. I am so sad and desperate because I miss Germany and my language. I miss it so much sometimes that it gnaws at my stomach like a cancer. I wish I could erase the feeling of emptiness I have had inside me since I came here, but it is very difficult, but I try every day to be better and more relaxed with this new world."

"I didn't know," I said, "that it was that bad for you."

"Only at times, and then it passes. I will get a hold of it and shake it free from me," she said defiantly. Her mood suddenly lightened, and her voice changed and became softer as wisps of nostalgia overcame her. Friede began to speak about her summer holidays before the war. "I miss the Baltic," she said, "and the fires on the beach in July or the long walks I used to take with my cousins in the woods around Hamburg, or my trips to the Black Forest and trips to Berchtesgaden."

"Soon, we'll go back to Germany," I said, making a promise I knew couldn't be kept.

"Sure," Friede said, "we will go one day again, and in the meantime I will get used to these cold toast days that you people call summer. No wonder everyone looks so sick in this town," Friede remarked, "you never get any long days filled with lusty heat."

"Sometimes there are days when it grows very warm in Halifax," I said wistfully. "It usually happens in August when the city closes for the holidays. The sun cooks the terrace houses," I said, "until they are like ovens with a fat goose cooking inside for Christmas. When those hot days come, the lucky ones have left town and are at the seaside, eating Blackpool rock and standing knee deep in channel water and shivering their backside off."

119

"Don't you find it strange," Friede asked me on another occasion, "that no one seems to sell flowers in this city?"

"There are a few shops that do," I said and changed the subject because I knew that few people within these city limits, even got flowers when they were dead. Garlands were reserved for the funeral hearses or for our more affluent members that were being carted off to the necropolis.

"People just don't fuss about with delicate things in Yorkshire," I said. "They don't get much time to themselves, and if they want to see nature, they go to a park or out on the moors for a ramble," I said as way of explanation.

"That is a very sad way to live your life," Friede said in a matter-of-fact tone. "Even the most desperate of Germans will still try to find some natural beauty to decorate their living space, no matter how difficult their circumstances may be."

"Well, at least we are different," I said, trying to reassure myself.

"Who, us?" Friede asked with a note of incredulity in her voice.

"Of course," I said. "There is no one else like us in this town. Besides you make my world better because you bring light and warmth to this tip of a county."

Friede beamed from the compliment and returned it to me when she remarked, "I am glad, at least, that you took Roy's suggestion and got a job at the Macintosh factory. It has taken away a lot of my worries."

"Mine, too," I said, "but I must dash or else I will be late."

Being employed at Mac's was an improvement in both conditions and wages compared to the machine shop. The toffee factory paid well because England's sweet tooth may have been capped by rationing, but our dominions were flourishing and eager to pay in hard currency for our confectionary. I was told by my managers that companies like Macintosh helped the nation square its debts with America.

Overall, it was a decent place to be employed that had many benefits, which greatly improved my day-to-day standard of living. One of them was a weekly sweet allotment that the company gave to its employees. Each one of us was given a weekly stipend of defective, broken, or misshaped sweets that we purchased at a discount.

The first time I was offered a bag of twisted malformed toffee in their wrappers, I had to ask what I was supposed to do with them.

"Don't go and gobble them up, you stupid git, because they're for trading for other stuff," said a fellow worker who stood beside me.

It wasn't long before I caught on to their enormous value in a country that had to make do with jam made from turnips.

I realised that the butcher, the baker, and the tobacconist were eager to trade me an extra rasher of bacon, a better cake, and a generous extra portion of tobacco, for sweet toffee. I felt like I was back in occupied Germany, where a carton of cigarettes bought a German family enough food supplies to keep them from starving to death.

With these Macintosh castoffs, I finally had something that other people coveted, and I made sure that I used it to improve our meagre food allotments.

One night after a corn beef hash supper, Dorothy said, "I think your Harry is on to something good. He will be known as the king of sweets in this house."

Friede grinned and said, "It's the same the world over, isn't it? You scratch my back, and I'll scratch yours."

For the first time since I left Germany, I began to feel content with the progress of my life and my employment. I went to work feeling that I was on the edge of a new world where stability ruled. I was liked by both my fellow workers and my supervisors, and even though my responsibilities were not taxing, I did my best to be noticed. The managers started to take an interest in my diligence and commitment to my job, which consisted of shunting pre-packed chocolate boxes to the loading docks.

"Won't be long now, Harry, and you'll be moving on to a new and better job with Mac's," said my supervisor. I thanked him, and he responded by telling me, "I mean it, the sky's the limit for a lad like you." His words of encouragement, made me glow inside for hours. *Finally,* I thought, *I'm moving up the ladder instead of my usual descent down and through a bolt hole.*

My only dilemma was that while my days were filled with pushing carts, cracking jokes, and expanding my connections and contacts, Friede's universe was shrinking to the very small and dense confines of our living quarters. For the most part, Friede spent her time while I was at work following a dismal routine of housework. When both Dorothy and I were at our jobs, Friede scrubbed down our damp and miserable terrace house, swept the front stoop, washed our clothing, and arranged and rearranged our bedroom. She even decorated it with small items she had brought from Hamburg to make it seem more familiar and comfortable for her.

Friede escaped the house every day by taking a solitary walk to the Carnegie Library to read a national newspaper. The information she gleaned from the headlines and analysis did nothing to assuage her already unsettled emotions, as the papers were filled with unsettling stories about the blockade against Berlin by the Soviets. Reporters and editorialists suggested another war was imminent.

Friede knew that if the U.S. and Russia went to battle, the war was going to be fought on German soil. She didn't need to look at a map to know that the Soviet Army was less than a day's march from Hamburg. Anxiety about another war and the immediate threat to her family, friends, and her city made her unhappiness even more acute. She confessed to me, "If there is war, I will not stay here; I will go home and be with my people."

"But this is your home," I said, perplexed.

"And Germany was my home for eighteen years; I will not abandon my people if Russia tries to gobble up the rest of Germany."

"It will never come to that," I said. "Everyone is tired of war, us, the Reds, and everyone else. Things will die down, believe me. We just have to wait and be patient."

Irma provided Friede some respite from her daily isolation as she called on her several times a week. However, the purpose of her visits was less about cheering Friede up and more about complaining about her life with Roy and his mother. "I married him because I thought he wasn't like any of the Italian men I knew. You know the ones I am talking about, Friede? They are as sensitive as a strong man at the circus. Well, Roy might not be like a bull in a china shop, but he is worse, far worse than any *bruto*. He is like a lamb on the way to the slaughter. He bleats happily until he gets the chop. He is a real mama's boy." Irma always ended her encounter with Friede by saying, "Sometimes I wish I never came to Britain. What kind of country can't make a decent cup of coffee? Is it so sinful to want an espresso?"

As the summer progressed, Friede plunged deeper into depression, but she shrugged off any suggestion that she was unwell. Friede tried to reassure me that these black moods were temporary. "It is nothing; they will pass because they always do."

However, much as she might be able to conceal her despondency during the daytime, night time was a different matter. Friede wasn't able to protect herself from her subconscious, and when she surrendered herself to sleep, all her emotions raged against her in the guise of night terrors. She'd wake screaming, shaking, and yammering discordant words in German. After the fit had passed, Friede eventually fell back into unconsciousness, but her limbs trembled involuntary as if she had palsy.

The only device Friede had to combat her melancholy was to write letters to her mother and friends back in Hamburg. At first she tried to be upbeat in her missives, but after a while her solitude got the better of her and she started to tell the truth to her mother about the less than ideal life she was leading.

Friede confessed in one letter to her mother that she found it incomprehensible how so many Brits lived in deplorable conditions and yet thought they were not the worse for it. How could these be the same people who came to Germany as cocky soldiers, occupiers, black market dealers, and speculators, but on their native soil they were timid towards authority and nonplussed by the ugliness of their cities, the poverty of their neighbourhoods, and the drabness of their lives?

Sometimes she wasn't sure if her mother believed her complaints about her loneliness and unhappiness. *I hardly sleep*, she wrote, *my nerves are shattered, and sometimes I am short tempered. Often I can be very cold towards my husband. I still believe in him and care for him deeply, but I am very uncertain how long I can remain in this cold and forsaken city.* It was, she wrote, a place so unlike anything she had ever known in her lifetime.

There was always a prompt reply from her mother and a stern rebuke from the mailman. "You got a German living here," said the mailman to Dorothy. "And you've got nasty thoughts living in your head," was her curt reply.

Maria Edelmann's response to her daughter never varied. She always cautioned her to be patient with her husband and her new country. Perhaps, she explained, the darkness was just an interlude to

123

daylight and happiness. She told her that times were hard everywhere and that Germany still suffered from both the war and the reconstruction and would do so for many years to come. Her mother cautioned that if there was to be another war, it was best that her daughter remained in Britain. It was a not a time for anyone to act foolishly, she advised.

As to the letters Friede wrote to her friends Ursula and Gerda, she made light of the English and their strange manners, their lack of refinement, their rough-around-the-edges attitude. She wrote of her growing friendship with Dorothy and the Italian war bride Irma. She always enclosed a cutting from a fashion magazine to show her girlfriends what the latest styles were in London. Friede assured them that she was having the best of times. She couldn't bear to think that her friends might think her a fool for marrying an Englishman and abandoning her country.

Lugubrious temperatures invaded Halifax in August and made life unbearable in our house and especially in our attic bedroom. The heat drove Friede to despair. "The papered walls," she lamented, "are weeping from the humidity." The heat, her loneliness and depression, and my decision to work through the factory shut down on a maintenance crew were becoming too much for Friede to bear.

At tea, Friede began to protest that everyone but her had a job.

"But you do," I said. "Look at what you must do around here in our home. It is more than sufficient to keep you occupied."

"No, I mean a real job outside of the house, like what you do," she said boldly.

Idiotically, I responded, "I should be able to provide for the both of us, and that should be the end of that."

"I need something to do outside of being a hausfrau. I need to feel that I have some value to this society," Friede said pleadingly.

I didn't know how to respond. I kept quiet and sipped on my beer, oblivious to her growing discomfort. I was blind to the dislocation that was developing inside her heart to me and to the way her life had turn out.

By September, Dorothy started to remark, "Your Friede is not well."

"What do you mean?" I asked. "She just is a bit glum because of the weather."

124

"Would you stop with that gobshite about the weather," Dorothy said angrily to me. "That girl is dropping weight like a jockey a week before the derby. She's not eating, and she's not talking. Even a man must realize that there is something wrong with her."

"Do you have any suggestions?" I asked helplessly.

"We must make an appointment for her to go see a doctor."

That evening, I approached Friede about seeing a doctor. She readily agreed, which surprised me, as did the condition she placed upon her visiting a physician. "I don't want you coming to the surgery. Do me a favour and just enjoy your Saturday morning, and I will be fine."

"Then who will take you?"

"I am sure Dorothy and Irma will be more than happy to accompany me, and then afterwards we can find a nice place to have tea and cakes."

Chapter Fifteen:
The Aunts of Barley Hole

Except for an occasional ripple of noise that came through the wall from our neighbour's dwelling, the house became as still as a pool of water after Friede and Dorothy departed. I loafed in the parlour and listened to an inane quiz show broadcast over the wireless box. There was a scent of wild flowers that lingered in the air. It was from Friede's perfume, and it teased my senses and made me remember my summer in Hamburg the previous year - when everything seemed possible.

I lit up a Player's cigarette and threw the spent match into the blackened grate. I inhaled deeply on the blue smoke and felt it bite into my chest. Exhaling, I went to the window and looked down the road and hoped to catch a glimpse of my wife before she departed into the ginnel, but she had already disappeared.

I sat down on the sofa, which smelled of tobacco, age, and decay, and started to blow smoke rings. Somewhere between the announcer making a double entendre and the live audience responding by bursting into applause, I became morbidly aware that I was just winging it through my marriage.

What do I know about women? I wondered. *I don't know the first thing about myself, let alone females.* I realised that in all my relationships, I had stumbled around in the emotional dark and hoped for the best. I was like a drunk trying to open up his front door at midnight and couldn't find the key hole. I was unable to understand the storm swirling around me because there was a tempest in my heart.

"This is becoming a real cock up," I said aloud. There was a sense of dread brewing up inside of me. I was now terrified that I had gotten Friede and myself into a trap that had no escape except through drink or death. The wheels were rapidly coming off our relationship, and I knew this doctor's visit would confirm what any fool could diagnose: Friede was unhappy with her life and her choice for a husband.

My dashing and cavalier ways in Hamburg had evaporated, and we now scrambled like the rest of working class Britain for our daily bread in an ugly mill town that had transformed its population into melancholic whingers. Nobody in my family, I realised, had ever been able to sustain a relationship. Every last one of them had ended up alone, or worse: stuck with their partner in the bitter dregs of a rotten marriage.

I just had to look at my parents' union to tell me that my family was unlucky in love and money. By the time my mum and dad had hit rock bottom, we were doing midnight runs to avoid doss house landlords and unpaid bills. They just couldn't cope with their disappointment in each other and in the world. As their son, I witnessed their love for each other spill out from their souls; it was like watching soldiers die from their wounds.

When it came to choosing a partner, even my sister Mary hadn't fared much better. She had married a man near the beginning of the war that had wooed her with two things that had been denied her as a child: affection and praise. The early promise of bliss evaded my sister, and instead she wound up like too many women and too many men: trapped, unhappy, and cheated of happiness. The war, the economy, and a feckless heart had turned her relationship into a marriage punctuated by bust ups and reconciliations. I imagined her love life was like a never-ending Ferris wheel that spun without pity from the top to the bottom.

Mary's fractious association with her husband made it difficult for my sister to communicate with me her despair. She had learned long ago to keep sorrow to herself, and I was no different with many of my problems. We tried to keep in touch by writing, but it didn't last long because after Mary alluded in a letter to the crumbling state of her marriage, she confessed that it might be some while before we could meet face to face because she knew that there was nothing I could do for her, or vice versa.

As that morning dragged on, I noticed I was running both out of cigarettes and the ambition to wallow in the emotional history of my family. *Got to get up and do something*, I thought. I stood up and was about to go sweep up the kitchen floor when I heard an unexpected knock at our front door.

I jerked the door open and found two elderly women standing in front of me. They both wore an identical scowl on their faces. It ran from the tip of their disapproving eyes down to their thin, annoyed lips. Their facades were so dour, I thought nothing could change their expressions, not even ten years of solid sunshine.

I wasn't sure who these unwelcomed guests were, but I shrugged off any idea that they were lost. They didn't look like they had ever been in need of direction or assistance in their lives. At first, I surmised that they were from the Jehovah Witnesses and were on a most unpleasant mission to sell me the miracles of Jesus.

"Sorry, ladies, but I'm not interested in God, charities, or orphans. Kindly take whatever you are peddling down the road."

Puzzled, they looked at each other, and then one of them addressed me, "We are not selling anything."

"Well, I don't know what you want, but I am sure I can't help you," I said.

"You can't help us," said the older one of the two, "but perhaps you can answer a question or two for us. Are you Harry Smith?"

"Yes."

"Harry Leslie Smith?"

"Yes," I said with impatience.

"Your sister is Alberta, now called Mary by some, but not by all."

"Yes," I said with some worry growing in my voice.

"Your father was Albert."

"Yes."

"May we come in?" said the younger of the two.

"We have something to discuss with you, and it is about your father," said the older one in a commanding voice.

Before I could assent to their request, the older woman impatiently blurted, "We don't have all day. We have to catch the bus back to Barnsley."

"Considering I was born and bred in Barnsley," I said sardonically, "I should have been more courteous. By all means, please come in?"

"Alright," said the older woman, "but we can stay for no more than ten minutes. I don't want to be left running for the bus. I have wasted too much time on this errand already, and I have much business to attend to at my pub."

"Yes, our stay must be brief," said the younger woman in a tone that implied that she had spent a lifetime dealing with her elder sister's hectoring manner

129

As they came into the small entrance of my house, one of the women said, "Aren't you going to ask us who we are?"

I managed to give them a half-sincere smile and said, "Ladies, I am chomping at the bit, so go on and tell me who you are."

"We are your aunts," they said in unison.

"My aunts?" I began to guffaw.

"This is no laughing matter," the younger said in rebuke.

"No, I suppose not," I responded. "You can rest assured that I am not amused to be your nephew. But considering you have come all this way to see me, please come sit."

I ushered them into the parlour and offered them a seat on the sofa. "Well, you two must tell me how we came to be related," I asked, uncertain as to whether or not I wanted to know their answer.

"We are your Dad's sisters."

"Excuse me," I said. "I must have misunderstood you," I said snidely. "I was not aware that my father had any sisters."

"He did," Harriet said, "and he also had many younger brothers."

"By gum," I sarcastically remarked. "And up until this day, I just sort of thought my father was a fondling, abandoned at birth because no one ever came to call when we flitted from one doss house to the next in Bradford."

The older lady sighed and said, "We loved Albert, your dad, but he broke with the family by going with your mum. It was an unforgivable transgression."

"Oh, Christ," I said with growing anger. "I don't know why you two are here, but if it is to open old wounds, then you can leave right now."

The younger woman became apologetic. "It is not our intention to cause you any distress because as they say: that is all water under the bridge."

The older one interjected, "Perhaps we can begin again. I am Mabel, and this is my younger sister Harriet. We have come a long way to pass on some news to you. Would you be so kind as to make us a cup of tea because it has been a long day for us two old ladies?"

I went to the scullery and filled a kettle full of water and put it on the hob, and then I began to mutter to myself that none of this boded well.

When the tea was ready, I brought it out to the sitting room. I lit up a cigarette and rudely blew smoke in their direction. Their intrusion into my life irritated me and stirred up in me an anger towards my father's irresolute family, who failed to be loyal to their own kind or show kindness to those who had been beaten soundly into the dirt by fate.

I looked dismissively at the two old ladies to see if I could find something in them that reminded me of my father's gentle but brooding soul. They both looked like they had been well taken care of in life, but their visages looked as hard as stone. Mabel looked to be in her seventies, while Harriet was perhaps ten years her junior. They appeared as proud and aloof as my dad, but they didn't seem to share his generous nature or his inquisitive mind. Nevertheless, the two women had some features in common with my father. They had his attractive eyes, elegant hands, and Victorian manners.

The women gently sipped their tea and nibbled on some biscuits. We were all silent, preoccupied by past events that we each endured from different perspectives. It was Mabel who finally broke our silence and said, "I was there when your Dad died in Bradford, at Saint Joe's Hospital, in 1943."

I didn't respond, and my aunt took this as an affirmation that I wished her to continue.

"He went painlessly," Harriet commented, as if this news were intended to reassure me or make me feel better about my father's pauper's exit from this mortal coil.

I was silent, and after a time I butted my cigarette out in the ashtray. "Small mercies," I said with some hostility in my voice.

"Your dad wanted you and your sister to have what money, whatever possessions he owned. Mind you, it's not much," said Mabel dismissively.

"Crumbs for a sparrow," chortled Harriet, who then looked around the room and took a mental accounting of where I stood - so to speak - on the ladder of life.

"But it was what your dad left you, and I wanted to respect your father's dying wish," Mabel concluded.

"My Dad died five years ago. That's a long time being dead, and it took you all these years to get in contact with me?"

Harriet put down her tea cup. It hit the saucer with some force. She muttered, "I can see the apple doesn't fall far from the tree in this field."

"I beg your pardon?" I responded with rising irritation in my voice.

"Your Da defied his family in 1914, and you seem to have his same independent and disrespectful manner when it comes to your elders. Your father was a fool to choose your mum over his family, and because of it, he was cast out from his kith and kin. He lost everything the day he married your mum: money, respect, eventually he couldn't even show his face in the village where he was born."

"Defied? Defied bloody what? You must be seriously taking the mickey out of me."

"Our family," said Mabel, "was a proud family, and your mum had no place in it; she was looking for an easy life."

"That's enough," I said. "Don't ever speak in that tone of voice to me about my mother or father or I'll chuck you out of this house by the scruff of your neck. Neither of you have the right to judge them, considering what they suffered for their so called 'transgression' against your kind. You lot are just a bunch of cold hearted, miserable bastards."

Mabel's expression darkened across her face as if she were about to unleash a tempest upon me, but Harriet interrupted her before she could strike. "We are just here to follow your father's last wishes; nothing more, nothing less. Once it is done, we can all go back to living our lives."

Mabel added, "As far as I am concerned, I didn't come here to stir up any old dirt. 'Leave the dead with the dead,' I say. I will give you your legacy, and then we will be off. Your father didn't leave much. There was no insurance or -"

I interrupted her, as I was growing irritated by her circumlocutions. "Mabel, I think it is safe to say that what his own people denied him and what the Great Depression stole from him, my Dad was busted both physically and financially when he clocked off."

"Yes," said Mabel with a distasteful note of superiority. "He didn't have much of value to sell, but here is your share." Mabel then handed me a handkerchief, which contained a small amount of coins.

132

"There is nine shillings and tuppence," she said, and then added, "please count it to make sure it is all there."

"I don't think it is necessary for me to count my father's Earthly worth, or the silverware, for that matter, after you have gone."

I took the money and held it tightly in my hand. I looked at my father's two sisters and said, "'Ashes to ashes,' quoth the parson."

The women concluded that our reunion was finished and stood to leave. I gathered their coats, and while they prepared to go, I asked - not expecting an answer - "Did he have any last words?"

Mabel said, "Not really. He was very sick. His lungs were shot from working in the mines, and his heart wasn't much better. It was like a clock that could no longer be wound because the mechanism was broken inside. I had gone to see him in hospital, but he was very weak but wanted to talk. So we spoke of long ago times when he was a miner at Barley Hole and our father ran the pub beside the pit. He wasn't afraid of death. In fact, I think he welcomed death. His only regret was how he lost touch with his children."

At this point, Harriet interjected and said, "Mabel, do not forget to tell him about what Albert said just before he died because it was most strange."

"Yes, you are right," responded Mabel. "The last word he said to me or anyone on this Earth was 'Babylon'. Honestly, I don't know what that means; he was not a religious man."

I smiled; I knew what it meant, but I was not going to tell them. I was not going to give up my father's secrets, my secrets, to these two old crows.

As the two ladies stood on our front stoop, I indifferently thanked them for their visit. I closed the door to them and shut the bolt, knowing that I was locking away that side of my family for good. *Let them rot in my memory as they've let us fester in the Depression*, I thought.

I sat back down on the couch and stared for a long while at the coins wrapped in a silk handkerchief. Outside, it had begun to rain, and it splashed against the window. I noticed I was out of cigarettes, and I scooped up my dad's legacy and slipped on my overcoat and went out to buy some cigarettes and beer at the off licence. When I stood in line to order, I thought about paying for my purchase with the coins from my dad's inheritance, but I stopped because something inside of me said this was not right.

On my way home, the cold spray from the rain washed away some of the dirtiness I felt after my encounter with my father's sisters. I returned to the parlour and turned the wireless box up loud and let it deafen me with swing music and sat down to drink my beer and stare at the loose change left to me by my father.

"Ta, Dad," I said and took a long swig from my beer. "I'll grant that you didn't leave me much, but then again, I never needed much from you. When I was four and you took me down the road for a plate of mushy peas, you bought my heart for a penny. Never you mind," I said to myself and started to weep. "I'll find Babylon, just like you promised me I would. Don't you remember, Da?" I said, talking to the coins. "It was when I was a lad and you let me look through your book, *Harmworth's History of the World*. I found all those beautiful pictures about the ancient wonders of the world and asked you, 'What is this place?', and you responded, *'It were a paradise, but one day, lad, when it is right as rain, you will travel far from these dales and cold moors. I feel it in my bones that you will see sights and wonders grander than those of ancient history.'"*

I wiped my tears dry with the cuff of my shirt. I realised that even though he was only in my life for a few brief years, his presence was worth a million pounds to me.

Chapter Sixteen:
Works and Days

It was late in the afternoon when Friede arrived back from her doctor's visit with Dorothy and Roy's wife Irma in tow. They burst into the house, excited and animated by their day out and that the weather had changed for the better.

"Finally, it feels like summer," Friede remarked to me as she kissed me hello. She began to relate how her day had transpired, following the appointment with the physician. "We just went to a posh tea shop near the council buildings, ate cakes, gossiped, and then went and window shopped at some of the better stores on Commercial Street."

"What happened at the doctor's surgery?" I asked nervously.

"I'll tell you everything in a while, but there is nothing to worry about. ."

It was at that point that I noticed that Irma was holding in her wire mesh bag a very large object wrapped in newspaper. She must have noticed my curiosity because she said in hasty fashion, "It's river trout. Don't ask how I got it," she said. "Just be glad that I will make you fish Italian style for your tea tonight." She then went into the kitchen with Dorothy to prepare dinner, and for the first few minutes I could hear them arguing and bickering back and forth about the proper way to gut and prepare a fish.

Friede and I sat down in the parlour and smoked from a packet of cigarettes that I had given her in the morning.

"Well, how did it go?" I asked nervously.

"I'm fine. The doctor is a marvellous woman who knows a lot about foreign cultures. She thinks I am suffering from nerves and shock."

"Shock?" I said with a note of surprise.

"Yes, the doctor says she has been seeing quite a lot of it recently, with all the refugees and foreign brides arriving in England. She believes that anyone who suddenly gets put into a different element is going to have trouble adjusting to a new environment. She thinks," Friede said in a serious tone of voice, "that I need to get out more and be more active with my mind and body."

135

"That's good," I said enthusiastically.

"There's more," Irma said, barging into the parlour. "Tell him everything because this woman doctor was no fool; she knows how a woman's heart and head ticks."

Friede explained, "She thinks I should get a job and also become more active within the community. If I do that, she says I will be less critical of myself and less nervous about the outside world."

"But where on Earth are you going to get a job?" I asked, perplexed. "You have no experience, and your English is far from perfect."

Angrily, Friede flashed her eyes at me and said, "And your German is far from ideal. So maybe you should help me more and criticise me less."

By this point, Dorothy appeared from the kitchen and brought with her a tray that contained a small bottle of gin and four glasses. "I think all of us need a splash of something, don't you?"

"I need a tidal wave," commented Irma, who then began to powder her face from an ornate compact. She started to complain bitterly about the Halifax air. "It makes your hair look like a flat tire."

Dorothy laughed and said, "That is why I always get two bottles of beer, one for me and the other for my head; nothing like a good stout to perk everything up."

Friede cupped her glass with both hands and swallowed the contents of her glass in one mouthful and remained quiet.

I was beginning to grow impatient with everyone in the room, and I blurted out sarcastically, "Does the doctor have any suggestion as to who might want to employ you?"

"As a matter of fact," Friede said, "She does. It would be a job helping with someone's children."

I scoffed at the notion and said, "I don't think you'll want to wipe any little nipper's bottoms around here, as they'll probably steal your purse."

"It is not around here," Friede said defensively. "It is one of the doctor's friends, but I can't remember the name of the street."

Dorothy assisted Friede by telling me, "It's Saville Park, but at the exclusive end."

"That's where the toff's live," I said derisively.

"I don't know what that means," Friede said. "It is just that the owner needs someone to look after his two small children because he is a widower."

Dorothy started to rub her thumb and forefinger together and said with a throaty laugh, "He's got pounds to spare because he owns a mill."

"The doctor said she would put in a word for me and I could go around next week and see if they could use me," Friede remarked.

I was taken aback; almost insulted by what Friede had told me because it seemed like it was an attack on my ability to provide for my wife. "I hope you told her thanks but no thanks because no wife of mine is going to be working in service. It's outrageous; what cheek," I said, feeling the gin burn as it went down into my stomach.

"I told her I am very happy to get the experience, and who knows where it will lead?" Friede said enthusiastically.

"I'll tell you where it will lead to: being promoted to char woman. We are better than that," I said, irritated.

Irma chimed in as if she were an overfed magpie. "It will be alright for Friede. If she doesn't like it, she can tell them to get...what is it you English say...stuffed. Besides, the doctor thinks Friede has something more to offer Halifax than dusting and polishing silver," she remarked provocatively.

"What is that?" I asked.

Friede took hold of my hand and said, "The doctor belongs to a woman's institute, and she wants me to give a series of speeches to her group and some church groups about life in Germany during and before the war. I think it was a wonderful suggestion because I can really help educate people about how Germans aren't bad people."

I was silent and decided that I wasn't going to disturb anymore of Friede's illusions that day by telling her that talking to church society groups was probably not going to be a help to anyone, but only reinforce their prejudices.

I had to admit one thing: Friede looked more relieved and at peace with her surroundings than I had seen her since she came to Britain. This was not what I planned for either of us when I came to these shores, that I'd be pushing crates of sweets for a living and that Friede would end up being depressed, lonely, and out of sorts. I wanted her to be happy and wanted myself to be happy. So, I accepted the inevitable and said, "If this is what you want, then I will support you."

I then began to tell Friede Dorothy and Irma about the unexpected visitors I had entertained in the morning.

"They came all the way from Barnsley to give you less than a pound from your dead dad's pocket book?" Dorothy said incredulously.

"Yes," I said. "It was almost a touching family reunification, except that I know they both had dollops of cash and were here to snoop and confirm that my dad and his immediate family were not of sound character."

"Well," retorted Dorothy, "they are lucky they didn't first go to your mum's house looking for you."

I started to laugh and said, "They would never have left Boothtown alive."

By the start of the following week, Friede started working at the mill owner's mansion as the governess to his four-year-old boy and a three-year-old girl. It was explained to Friede that the children needed extra attention, as they had recently lost their mother to cancer. The mill owner told Friede that for the present she would not receive any wages. "You're on sufferance," he said while winding an ancient pocket watch.

Friede was confused and asked him to explain to her when exactly she was to receive a wage.

"As soon as I say that you are competent in your position. In the meantime, think of this as a learning experience, like school."

The mill owner did, however, concede to pay her bus fare. He also allowed Friede to take her meals with the family rather than the rest of the household staff.

"That's outrageous," I said to Friede when she told me that she was not being paid for her labour.

"I'm sure it won't be long until he pays because his children are very fond of me," Friede said hopefully.

By the end of September, Friede had begun making her speeches to the woman's clubs around Halifax on weekends. I escorted Friede to small church halls, where she addressed elderly and middle age women about life under Hitler. Friede's speech was always an impromptu remembrance of life in Hamburg. Her theme always stressed her city's cultural diversity before the war, the shared loss that all women endure during the war, and the deprivations German citizens experienced during the Allied Occupation.

These talks did an enormous of amount good for Friede's self-esteem. Sharing her experiences as a witness to Nazism, Friede thought that those who heard her speeches might have a greater appreciation of what it was like to live in a totalitarian society. "I want them to understand that Germans are no different than any other race of people. Some are very good, others ordinary, and some are beyond humanity's reach because of their innate wish to do evil."

Being a governess, however, proved to be less rewarding to her self-regard than making speeches to the local women's associations. Friede grew increasing frustrated by the mill owner's reluctance to pay her a wage. There was something else that made her grow concerned about the mill owner's true intent. She found it unsettling that he tried to present gifts of lipstick and, expensive foodstuffs to her and that he also offered to drive her home in his expensive car.

Friede always declined, but as the mill owner's advances became more forward, she grew more nervous about going to her workplace. Friede also noticed that other members of the staff began to ostracise her because she was permitted to take meals upstairs with the family while they had their tea downstairs. "It isn't proper," said the cook to her one day about this favoured eating arrangement.

I started to feel put out and jealous over the amount of time she spent with the mill owner and his children. Friede was at the mill owner's house for close to twelve hours a day, six days a week, and as I pointed out to her, "This is just madness because you aren't even being compensated for it." Friede attempted to assuage my wounded pride and her own misgivings by stating, "He has promised to start paying me very soon, and he thinks I am perfect for the job. Just be patient, and you will see; he will give me a wage."

When Friede's birthday arrived in October, she asked the mill owner whether he might consider her sufficiently trained to be paid a wage. He said that he didn't think it was the right time but that it would be soon. Friede told him she was disappointed by his answer, whereupon he said there was something that she could do for him that would guarantee her a wage by the end of the week.

"What's that?" she asked excitedly.

"Kiss me, and I will definitely think much better of you," responded the mill owner.

After the owner made the remark, Friede's face grew red in anger and shame. She felt like a fool because she had been tricked by a rich man who wanted to take advantage of a young woman.

The mill owner asked again if she would kiss him.

Friede lashed out at him, "You are such an insignificant man. I'd slap you, but I don't want to soil my hands by hitting your face. It is just shameful that you wanted to try to take advantage of me."

After her outburst, the owner said in a calm tone that he no longer required her services.

"How dare you," Friede said, "sack me. The moment you made me such an outrageous proposal, I stopped being your employee. I will not work for a reptile."

The owner was not fazed by Friede's outrage, and it seemed to her that he had experienced similar rebuffs from other domestics. He did warn her that "it would be prudent to let this matter go no further. The scandal," he said, "will only harm you and your husband. After all, who is going to believe that a respected businessman, a pillar in the community, would be mucking about with a filthy German?"

Friede stormed out of the house and said to him before she left that he was a swine and she pitied his children for having such a dishonourable father.

Chapter Seventeen:
Movement

In its customary fashion when November's arrived, the temperature fell; the sun went into exile and rain dropped like shrapnel from a coal black sky down onto Halifax's cobbled streets. My spirit began to taper from the lack of light and the desperation of finding that one day led to another that was exactly the same as the last. The only element of my work day that I relished was the end of my shift at Macintosh's which ended at half four.

When I was done for the day, I crossed the factory's gates with a hundred other employees. Everyone was dressed the same: workman's jacket, cap and scarf. Around us there was the smell of tobacco that stuck like treacle to the outside air as worker after worker sparked up a cigarette and exhaled dirty smoke. Few of us spoke, so the only sound came from the weary crush of our boots against the stone pavement.

By the time we'd reach the end of the roadway, the stream of workers divided and subdivided as each employee rushed to catch a bus to their home. Not one of us looked back to the looming brick monolith where we had toiled since sun up. We were like caribou migrating to their winter grazing grounds who stared straight ahead in the direction of food and rest.

Guy Fawkes was the only night when Halifax appeared festive, warm, and accommodating, during that month. For one short night, we were granted an ephemeral camaraderie with strangers as the neighbourhood commemorated a centuries old conspiracy against the crown that was thwarted.

"It looks like they want to burn down the neighbourhood," Friede remarked, when she witnessed the celebration for the first time

"This is all in good fun, a way for the young ones to blow off steam," I said. "When I was a lad, we'd spend days collecting wood for the fires that were lit for the Guy Fawkes commemoration, and sometimes we'd fight other children from different streets for the best piece of timber for our bonfire."

"It is a strange festivity," Friede concluded.

I laughed and said, "I think it is one of our best. Guy Fawkes celebrates not only the death of a traitor, but gives two fingers back at the winter to come. Everyone that is out tonight looks happy, and I know it might be the beer in their bellies that gives their cheeks a rosy hue, but at least for this short time, people feel like they belong to a community. Better still, they can toss all their anger towards their bosses, the government, or their spouses onto the fire and say 'Cheerio.'"

A couple days after the fiery celebration, it was evident that winter was coming. I smelt it in the outside air, and I saw it on the pessimistic expressions of people on the street. It was everywhere except on the advertisements that covered the sides of the local buses. The cold gloom was at our border, while hope, joy, and optimism readied themselves for hibernation.

There was nothing we could do to prevent the frost, the inhospitable temperatures, or the sunless days but bundle ourselves up in our winter coats, light a cigarette, take refuge in a cinema, and watch the latest flick from America. If we felt sufficiently flush or down in the dumps, we found a pub that had an abundant supply of fuel and song to make us feel warm in the company of fellow lost souls.

As the light began to fade across the West Riding and the nights grew longer and more desolate, Friede's sense of isolation became more acute. Her letters home were more desperate and more frequent, and she pined for a quick response to her missives from both her friends and her mother. "I miss having people to talk to in German," she confessed to me.

"I know," I replied, "but what about your new friends, Irma and Dorothy? Surely, they must be of some comfort to you?"

"They are," she said pensively and hesitated. It was as if she were searching for the correct word to describe her ambivalence to these new relationships. "They are very good people, but we only share today. They can't ever replace my childhood friends and what we experienced together. I know I am building knew memories with Irma and Dorothy, but it is altogether different than what I have with those I love back in Germany. I feel I can't fully confide in either Dorothy or Irma because they will judge me without knowing me."

"How so?" I enquired.

"Irma and Dorothy are friends of circumstance, like when you meet people on a train journey; the relationship only lasts as long as the shared voyage. I believe each of us very soon will arrive at different destinations, and when that happens we will say goodbye."

Friede also admitted that she sometimes felt awkward around those two women.

"Why?" I asked.

"Irma is too opinionated," she said, "especially about her husbands' shortcomings. She airs what you English say is too much dirty laundry in public. Must she always try to humiliate him?" she asked. "I would never do that to you or to anyone I cared about. Certain things must be private between a man and woman."

"What about Dorothy then?" I asked, perplexed.

"She is a wonderful woman and has been very kind to me. But Dorothy has an order, a way of doing thing that cannot be broken; everything must be done in an English way. It is like she wants to strain me in a sieve like a boiled cabbage to get rid of my entire German heritage."

Friede did concede that despite their imperfections, these two women were sincere in their affection for her, and her for them. Moreover, as time went on, she began to depend on Irma for many things. Her Italian friend was loyal, if somewhat operatic about the stress and strain of living in Britain. Irma's theatrics were a way of coping with her unfolding life. She had to find some way to make sense of her arrival in Halifax and her changed circumstances.

There was something indefatigable about Irma. She never grew tired of complaining about her present life or providing Friede with endless suggestions and solutions for both her mundane and metaphysical problems. It didn't matter what the subject, Irma had an opinion. It was especially pronounced when it came to hairstyles, fashion, or make-up. Irma concluded she must know everything because she spent her weekends devouring London society magazines. As for home economics, Irma believed she was also the best judge of what made a perfect roast, stew, or soup. It was unfortunate that her husband's sense of taste was as acute as a ruminant. If it weren't a rock bun or sugary tea, he couldn't discern what it was. "I could serve him porridge every day," Irma lamented, "and he would think it was foie gras."

Irma didn't just hold opinions on domestic relationships, clothing, and food; she also had loud and often contentious beliefs about urban renewal for Halifax itself. "Sweep it all into the dust bin, and walk away from it. When they made this town, they squeezed all the happiness out of the Earth like it was pulp from an orange."

Friede found Irma sometimes overwhelming, and at other times she admired her friend's energy, self-confidence, and sarcasm; however, Friede realized that Irma's friendship came with barbs and thorns. Irma was incapable of holding a confidence, and it didn't matter if she had high or low regard for someone, as soon as they were out of earshot, they were turned into a target for criticism and derision.

Despite Irma's grand airs, she was a pragmatist at heart. She understood that her pride prevented her from leaving her husband and returning to Naples because she feared being labelled "a broken woman" by Italian society. She realized that marrying a foreigner might have been a mistake, but unlike Lot's wife, she was not going to look back. Her life, for better or worse, was now in Yorkshire, and she wasn't pleased by this strange twist of fate. Nevertheless, Irma decided that it would be foolish not to try and get as much material comfort and satisfaction that Halifax had to offer her.

Irma was also clear to everyone, including her husband, that although her house in Halifax was considered lower middle class by British standards, it was a giant step down in society for her. She knew that the only way she was ever going to get what she wanted was by going out and taking it because "my husband is such a donkey that he'd never find a bushel of carrots unless it dropped right in front of his face."

So, Irma demanded that Roy speak to the management at Macintosh's. She wanted him to inveigle a position for her at the factory. "I don't want anything fancy; just a job so I can get out of this house and away from your mother."

It took one sit down with a manager for Irma to be hired. Finally, she believed that with this new job, she was freed from depending on Roy's household accounting. After she started working, she told Friede, "I feel like I am my own person again. The only way us women are going to get ahead in this country is if we

144

wear the trousers. It is not so great a job, but I now make my own money, and I can spend it how I please."

Irma encouraged Friede to do the same and get a job at Macintosh. "You'd be perfect there, and if you worked there, I'd have someone to talk to that understands me and doesn't think I am a bloody foreigner out to steal their precious British life."

Friede contemplated Irma's suggestion, but she had lost a great deal of her self-confidence when the mill owner had propositioned her. She mused to Irma that she didn't feel that she had the experience or that they would take kindly to hiring a German.

"Look," Irma said, "they hired me, and I'm Italian. So why wouldn't they hire a German girl? All they need to do is take on a Japanese girl, and they have the entire Axis underneath their roof. Besides, they'll take you as sure as they employed me because your husband works there and they like him. Harry could be a foreman in no time because of the way he takes on extra work. Anyways, you are not lazy like some of these local English girls that work in the factory who are always going for their cigarette breaks."

When Friede told me about Irma's suggestion, I thought it was a very good idea. "Your English is very good. It would be a good introduction to working in Britain," I remarked.

Friede was still not convinced, and it took much discussion and persuasion until she finally relented and went for an interview. Friede was interrogated by a spinster of indeterminate age but pleasant demeanour that worked in the toffee factory's administration office. It wasn't a long or comprehensive interview, but more of a chat to see if Friede was sufficiently British to work for the country's best toffee company. It seemed her youth and her ability to create a facade of enthusiasm for life in Halifax was adequate for the spinster. Friede was given a position on the chocolate assembly line; it was where most new female employees started and ended their working careers.

"What was it like?" I asked her while we walked home after her first day.

"It is a lot better than being alone in the house all day," Friede said with a breezy laugh. "It is certainly not difficult, but I am sure after a while it will get monotonous." Her tone grew more contemplative, and she said, "I never saw myself working in a factory;

I always thought I'd be doing something far more adventurous than that, but I am so happy to be out of the house."

Friede worked from Monday to Friday at Mackintosh's. She was required to wear a white smock, peaked hat and delicate white gloves while she stood at the side of a conveyor belt and wrapped chocolate confections into brightly covered foil paper. It was hard on her legs and back to stand in one fixed robotic position for hours at a time, but she didn't mind. "I feel like I am finally doing something and we are moving ahead," she confessed to me.

Irma worked on the line beside her, and although they couldn't speak to each other until break, they looked up now and then and shared a laugh or a sigh. Irma soon discovered that working nearby her and Friede were two other women who were not English born. She soon befriended these two expats and was surprised to learn that, like Friede, they were German. "Imagine that," said Irma. "Macintosh's is a regular United Nations."

"I don't think four women from continental Europe out of thousands counts for much diversity," Friede responded.

When Irma introduced her to the other German women, Friede was at first disappointed by her encounter with them. She realized that outside of a shared native tongue, the three had little in common. "They are really not my type," Friede confessed to me one day as we rode the bus home. She explained that one of the women was named Margaret and was much older than her. "She's forty-two and hasn't been in Germany since the 1936 Olympics."

"How did she get here then?" I asked, puzzled.

Friede explained to me that when Margaret was young, she ran off to Britain with an Anglo-Indian she'd met in Berlin. Eventually, the two ended up in India and lived a life of relative comfort before the war. At the beginning, it was a blissful existence, and Margaret resided in a beautiful house where she was waited on by a myriad of servants. Each summer, they travelled like royalty to her husband's retreat in the mountains to escape the tropical heat.

After giving her husband two children, the allure of life in India began to wear on Margaret. She felt trapped by a thousand years of tradition, which made her life as the wife of an Anglo-Indian as pleasant as life for a bird in a gilded cage.

146

Eventually, she left her Indian husband and took up with an Irish prison guard named Patrick. He was a tall, strapping man who didn't ask much from Margret or her two children. All Patrick wanted was that his modest household was run as efficiently as the native prison where he was employed. He liked to think that while he oversaw native miscreants weave by hand enormous wool carpets, Margret was at home running a similarly tight ship with their penny-a-day house servants.

After the Empire fell, so did their dreams of living life large on the backs of Indian servants and the ancient customs of the Raj. A year after India became independent; Patrick, Margaret, and her two children boarded a ship that sailed to Liverpool with the diaspora of Britain's lost colony.

When they arrived in Britain, the couple moved to Halifax because Patrick had some very distant relatives who promised them a free place to stay while he got back on his feet. Patrick took up his relatives' offer and they moved into digs that were in a rougher neighbourhood than ours.

Both Margaret and Patrick were able to get employment at Macintosh's because he had impeccable references as an upright custodian in the Indian penal system. It was neither the job nor the life Margaret had bargained for and she was despondent over her changed circumstances when Friede befriended her.

"Why is she down?" I asked. "It seems they got out of India just when things were turning sour."

"She is nostalgic for the easy life they had in India, and the same goes for her husband Patrick, who feels cheated by their present standard of living."

I started to laugh and said, "I am sure it was quite a let-down for them and the rest of Britain's insignificant functionaries who had to return from India. They all got the chop after decades of screaming 'Chop, chop' to people they thought were beneath them. Now look at them: they had to come home to mother England and begin life anew as non-entities in unremarkable cities and towns."

The other German woman who worked on the chocolate wrapping assembly line had a less exotic journey to her new life in Britain. She, like Friede, met and married a British serviceman, but asides from that they had nothing in common. The woman's name

147

was Ingrid, and she was twenty-two, and by the way she stood or walked, it seemed that tragedy was a constant companion that dragged her down.

Ingrid had been born in the industrial Ruhr area of Germany. Her family were workers, and by the rheumatic look that haunted her eyes, it seemed that she had experienced the unpleasantness of poverty and want since she was small. It wasn't hard to guess that she had married the first foreign soldier who showed an ounce of kindness to her because she was like a flower in need of water to bloom.

It wasn't likely that Ingrid was going to get the care and attention she needed from the man she married. He was a man who had experienced his own troubles and thought it best to keep them tightly packed away. He locked them in his soul, and the hurt and anger only came out if he drank too many pints down at his local. Her husband kept most emotions under wraps, except for his profound dislike for the Germans.

"Even if there hadn't been a bloody war, I'd still not like the flipping Germans. Miserable bunch of bastards, and if you hear them talk in German, it sounds like two dogs chewing over a bone. I wouldn't be caught dead learning their language 'cause English is good enough for anybody that matters."

After several social encounters at her house with the two Germans, Irma began to find them bothersome. She didn't refrain from telling them what she thought about their moaning, which she believed was pedestrian compared to her complaints. Once, she lectured them both and said, "If I wanted to listen to Wagner, I would have asked my husband to buy me the record."

"Those two are a dreary lot," she remarked to Friede one morning as they walked to the tea room at work. "But I suppose until we meet up with more interesting foreigners, they are the only friends we have because the other English girls always give us a wide berth."

It was true that there was a certain amount of xenophobia amongst the factory workers. The men and women who worked there had been taught from birth to be suspicious of people who were not from their neighbourhood or their class. Some employees had a hard enough time finding common ground with somebody from Lancashire, let alone from countries that had once been our

148

enemy. The war for some was as fresh as the smell of bread baked in the morning.

Even though there were less than a dozen women that worked at Macintosh's that were from Germany or Italy, some of the more obdurate workers considered them potential fifth columnists. "They're over 'ere now, the Jerries and Ities, and living high off the hog."

"They are taking all the good jobs away from us and thumbing their noses at us while they do it."

"Gawd, get a load of them and their funny way of speaking and their special airs. Bloody foreigners! Why did we win the war for them to come over here and take everything from us?"

Friede didn't seem to be upset by the small prejudices she endured, but it did add to her sense of separation and her homesickness, which became more acute as we approached the Christmas Season. A sense of uncertainty also began to pervade our household when Dorothy announced to us that her philandering husband had washed up on our shore like a bit of drift wood. "Don't want to cause any alarm bells, but we are getting back together again," she said in the breathless and dreamy voice.

"I see," I remarked. "I suppose that means Friede and I will have to look for a new place to stay."

"Not right away," Dorothy replied, trying to be conciliatory. "He won't be moving home until after New Year's, so if you can arrange to be moved out sometime in January, it would be smashing," she said.

I noticed when she now spoke about her husband; her voice took on a school girl's pitch. It was as if she were speaking of a different person rather than the man who had caused her so much heartache and hardship. I concluded he was to be reprieved because loneliness makes cowards of us all.

Having to move again was making Friede nervous, and she said, "We are like gypsies."

"We'll land on our feet because we always do," I said.

Friede wasn't satisfied by my response and said, "I don't know. Maybe we will, maybe we won't, but what I am really scared about is what is going on in Germany." She then spoke about the never-ending gloomy reports she heard on the wireless about her native country.

"There's continuous tension along the border that separated Soviet occupied East Germany from Allied occupied West Germany. Those people who are trapped in Berlin or enslaved in Dresden are no better off than France was under Nazi occupation," she said tearfully. "I don't want to see another war, a battle between East and West fought on German soil, especially with those atomic devices which are the work of the devil."

It was an uncertain Christmas we stumbled into that year because conditions in Britain seemed to be forever frozen in permafrost of rationing and economising. Shop windows were papered with cheerful but faded colours, and everyone looked hurried or angry or sad while they meandered towards the holidays.

On a couple of occasions, Friede and I even went out to a pub for an evening's entertainment. Insides these smoking enclaves, salutations and good wishes were washed down with fresh beer and risqué Christmas carols. After a pint or two, Friede and I would make our way home and talk of the Christmas we spent together in Hamburg.

"It was beautiful, wasn't it?" Friede asked.

I didn't know how to answer, so I remained silent

A few days before Christmas, I went shopping for gifts and ran into my brother Matt on Commercial Street. I took him for a beer at a pub and wished him a Happy Christmas. I also told him that I wouldn't be swinging around to our mother's house anytime soon. He said he understood and then related how my mother was now in a constant state of simmering boil.

"The dragon will spit fire," he said, "at the drop of a penny. Yesterday, she gave her man Bill a good hollering, and then she threatened to kill herself. But after I went looking for a knife for her, the old duck calmed down and asked me to fetch her a cuppa."

Roy and Irma invited us over to their house for Christmas Eve and Christmas Day. We gladly left our tiny garret for the comforts of their more spacious house and the good cooking of his mother. It was not a Christmas that Friede had ever experienced because in Britain, Christmas Eve was not the focal point of the holiday; instead we spent it in a very English manner: we ate a buffet supper, listened

150

to the gramophone, sipped on sherry, and were in bed before midnight.

When we were safely wrapped underneath our warm blankets, the church bells began to peel. It was the start of Christmas Day, and I heard Friede sigh. I knew she was thinking of Germany and how her mother and friends would be drinking champagne and opening gifts and looking at the glow coming from candles burning from the Christmas tree.

Chapter Eighteen:
The End of the affair

During the dying days of 1948, my relationship with Friede started to unravel. Our love was forged in the cauldron of Germany's terrible hunger winter, but Britain's season of discontent tore apart the delicate bonds that held our marriage together. After living too long in the bleak and hopeless world of England's working class, our affections began to cool. Our hearts had grown cold in an unattended hearth as if they were like orphaned embers of coal. The passion that had stoked our love ran out of oxygen because we lived in society's murky depths, where sunlight rarely shined. By Christmas day our marriage neared the beginning of its end.

There was a cold draft that wafted through our empty house when we returned home from Roy and Irma's yuletide gathering. I noted that the Christmas cards looked derelict, strung across the mantel in the cold and dark parlour. We lit some candles and started the fire, but Friede and I weren't able to thaw our chilly emotions that we had developed for each other. Neither of us was sure when these feelings of animosity had come upon us, but I was certain that they were not soon to pass. With Dorothy gone to her mother's, we had free license to argue from sun up to sundown with only the hiss from the gas lights to distract our thoughts from our disintegrating union.

By Boxing Day, Friede and I were worn down from quarrelling. We argued over trifles, from whether the room was too cold or too hot to why the tea always tasted like tepid water with a hint of rust. We no longer spoke to each other in civilized tones, but used surly and wounded inflections to express our emotions, which were divided neatly into two separate camps: wounded pride and aching heart.

Irritable, irritated, or unfeeling was how we responded to the other's rebukes. There appeared to be no solutions or map for us to save our relationship. It was more convenient and momentarily satisfying to slam a door in blinding exasperation or cut into the other with sarcasm and impatience rather than be honest with ourselves. Neither of us wanted to admit that we shared some blame

153

for the mess we had made of our marriage, nor did we want to admit that our marriage was failing from a thousand disappointments, a thousand dreams washed away because of a fractured economy, and a thousand promises broken because we never felt that we could get ahead of the past. Time was no balm because we knew it never wavered or stopped; it moved onwards and left our illusions of a prosperous and momentous life on the kerb side, waiting to be collected by the dustman.

Between rising from bed and going down to sleep, we sought to escape each other's company or touch. When by chance we brushed up against the other, it was as uncomfortable as when two boats slip their moorings in a harbour and scraped sides. It was preferable to be apart from each other rather than endure moments of mutual reproach that seemed to burrow underneath our skin and fester in an ooze of raw emotion.

I found no consolation, nor did Friede, by the fact that our friends, acquaintances, and millions of other people on this mirthless island were as unhappy as us. From the proverbial Mr. and Mrs. Jones in Wales to Mr. and Mrs. Moir in Aberdeen, everyone was making do on low wages and high expectations for a better future that never seemed to materialize.

It was despairing to me that despite the Labour government's revolution in education, medicine, or their attempts to create better housing for the working class, it was never going to immediately improve my generation's struggle for financial stability. Prime Minister Attlee was laying the foundations for a better tomorrow with guidance from William Beveridge, but that dawn was far off in the future. As for the present, I knew I was on my own and the keys to the kingdom were going to be forever denied me, no matter who ruled Britain.

Our financial problems went beyond Britain's stratification of the classes and division of labour based on region. The system's inherent corruption and bias towards rewarding the rich and strangling the poor of any hope for change poisoned my courage to dare to be different and demand a different fate. At one point before the close of the year, Friede left me speechless when she asked out of abject frustration, "How are we supposed to get ahead in this country when everything is divided so unfairly?"

I put my hands up in surrender because it had always been that way and was not likely to change in my lifetime. "It is the way things have always been done. The loaf is never cut straight, so you have to be crafty to get a bit of crust at the end."

Friede looked at me as if I were a child and remarked with irritation, "This country is never going to get back on its feet if the majority of the people believe that they are damned if they do and damned if they don't."

"Well, where are things working?" I asked sarcastically.

"Pretty well everywhere else. Just look at America: they are constantly evolving and growing stronger by the day. It seems that people have the same jobs as here, but they are paid a decent salary and can afford to live in nice places, unlike England, where no one seems to have a nice place to live but the rich."

"Don't talk to me about the Yanks," I said. "They are a bigger country with more raw materials than us."

"Fine, I won't talk about them," Friede said, "but I will talk about Germany. Hamburg is rebuilding itself, and people are working again and making good wages. In Germany, there is room for anyone that wishes to work, but it seems the same cannot be said about England."

"I don't want to hear one more bloody word about your country. We live in Britain now, and there is nothing that can change that. All we can do is try and keep our chins up and work harder until someone recognizes our efforts."

"You're mad," Friede said, "if you think anyone in Halifax is going to recognize your drive or ambition."

After our tenth or twelfth disagreement about getting ahead or making do, I switched off and grew cold to any of Friede's entreaties. I also tuned out any pain I caused her. I rationalized that if she was prepared to snipe at me, then I was more than willing to return the animosity in naked and cutting barbs that stung her heart.

My emotional withdrawal made Friede become colder towards me. We orbited each other like frozen, lifeless satellites made of volcanic rock until we slipped from each other's gravitational pull and drifted off into our deep dark space. Friede found refuge in writing letters to her mother and friends in Germany and fantasizing about

155

returning to Germany, while I dreamed about getting myself sorted out in Halifax.

It took me and Friede until New Year's Eve to decide that for appearance sake, it was wise to call a truce to our fighting. We didn't want anyone to suspect that our marriage was in serious trouble, despite the fact that everyone we were acquainted with had an imperfect and barely functioning relationship.

We spent the thirty-first at a dinner party hosted by Roy and Irma. It was attended by our usual crowd of friends: Margaret, Patrick, Ingrid, Norman, and also included Roy's elderly mother and lame aunt. It was a gentle gathering that resembled a Tuesday evening card night for middle aged couples rather than a get-together for young people celebrating the start of a new year.

Throughout the evening, we amused ourselves with inane small talk and harmless jokes. We drank weak gin fizz and played charades. When miming cues to our partners became too tiresome, even for Roy, we switched on the wireless and smoked cigarettes. Everyone wore comical New Year's hats, and because we were dressed in suits and fancy dresses, everyone looked like they were from the middle class. I wasn't sure if we were dressed like that because we wanted a night of make believe or we hoped that one day through our industry and acumen to be part of that society.

By about nine o'clock, Friede and Irma looked bored by the sluggish route the party was taking to get towards midnight. Irma scowled and pouted, while Friede looked preoccupied. I imagined that her mind was filled with visions of former New Year's or by promises I'd made in the past and hadn't kept. When Roy's mother and elderly aunt retired to their beds at eleven, Friede suggested, "We should all at least have one dance this evening, don't you think?"

Patrick shrugged off the suggestion and went back to eating his cake, while Norman looked aghast as if he had been invited to walk on hot coals and mumbled, "Not in my bloody lifetime." Irma just shrugged her shoulders and said, "Watching Roy dance is like watching a dog walk on ice."

Friede was not deterred, and she insisted that if no one was interested, she was going to dance by herself. The wireless began to play an upbeat tune, and Friede took my arm and dragged me up to dance. While we did a fox trot, the women sitting around us

156

applauded while the men guffawed. Just as the tune was about to fade into static, our eyes met. For a second, we both recognized our old selves and remembered why we had fallen in love with the other. That moment of clarity lasted as long as the final chord from the song, and once the music stopped our hearts returned to stone.

After the song ended, we stood uncomfortably in the middle of the living room, and we were not sure what to do next. It was Irma who solved our dilemma by jumping up from her chair and saying at the top of her voice, "Now it's my turn to dance with Friede."

I sat down and noticed Ingrid sitting across the room from me. She was kneeling beside her husband like an unhappy lap dog while he was gruffly ensconced in a comfortable chair. Her face wore a sad and longing expression as she watched the two women gracefully move across the carpeted floor. It wasn't long before Friede also registered Ingrid's melancholy, and she broke from Irma's embrace and reached over to her and pulled her up to dance while Irma followed suit and danced with Margaret.

At midnight, the church bells across Halifax rang and ushered in the last year of the decade. We all rushed out into the cold night and air to announce the New Year from the top of our lungs. The women hugged each other while the men shook each other's hands and wished the normal glad tidings for 1949. I went over to Friede and kissed her with lukewarm passion. Silently, I hoped that this coming year was not going to prove to be as miserly and disappointing as the last.

Both emotionally and physically, January felt as remote and frozen as a season on the moon. We endured the month like shipwrecked sailors in an open boat and shivered through the cold, wet, and bleak days. Our New Year's armistice lasted no longer than our return to work and our resumption of our ordinary lives. We tried to avoid arguments by ignoring each other. We uttered few words from the moment we rose in the morning until we went to bed.

If we did speak, it was about mundane matters and little else. My words to her were not profound or sensitive, but commonplace. I asked about whether a shirt had been darned, and she would affirm in the positive or negative.

The only subject that concerned both of us was the matter of finding new accommodations.

By the third week of January, Friede began to ask every night over tea whether I had found us a new place to live.

The incessant question about when and where we were to move to, irritated me because the dilemma hung over me like the proverbial sword of Damocles. I thought, *why does she have to keep hectoring on it about this bloody move?* I responded curtly that, "Something will turn up."

"You always say that," Friede remarked, then began to speak to herself in German.

After a couple weeks, my luck changed on the housing front, and I finally found something that looked promising in the local newspaper. It seemed ideal, almost too good to be true because it was an actual detached house for let in a better neighbourhood. When we went to look at it, we thought that it was paradise, and I hastily paid the rent and made arrangements for us to move to our new home.

When we moved into our new accommodations, I thought the change was going to be ideal for our relationship because it was located in Hipperholme, on the outskirts of Halifax. It was an area, I believed, where Friede and I might try to rekindle our romance and find that love we once had for each other. It was the most respectable neighbourhood I had ever lived in during my life in Britain. The estate even had a well-to-do ring to its name and was called Tennyson Bungalows.

The home even had an indoor toilet and a proper bath, which was a luxury I had never experienced while living in Yorkshire. It was Heaven for me, even though the rent was too high and it took all of Friede's salary to pay for it. I didn't even mind that we had to share the house with the owner, his wife, and their two young daughters. Friede and I both thought that by living in better accommodations in this rural backdrop, we might be able to recreate the ingredients that had made our romance in Germany blossom; instead, the reverse happened, and no fruit was born from our time in Hipperholme - it only accelerated the progress of the disease that was killing our marriage.

158

As the months passed and February changed to March and the days grew longer, our estrangement became more fixed and acute. We fell into a habit of observing the rituals of marriage without much enthusiasm, like churchgoers on Sunday that made the sign of the cross whilst thinking of their afternoon roast. Each day was no different than the day before we got up from our bed like strangers, sharing a kip and eating breakfast in silence. We walked down the street to the bus stop in silence, and when our ride arrived, we jumped on the bus and sat together in silence. When we reached our stop, we climbed off and walked to the entrance of Macintosh's, where we separated to go to our separate work areas. I'd give Friede a peck on the cheek, whereupon she'd turn to me and say, "I'll see you at the end of the day."

When our shift was over, we returned as we had come: on a crowded commuter bus. Although there was noise all around us, between us there was a fog of silence until we reached our stop at the bottom of the street, which led us to Tennyson Bungalow. During dinner, we made passionless small talk or stared at the food on our plate until we found peace by listening to the wireless, which drowned out the sour thoughts that had collected in our minds.

At lights out, we went to our bed and drew the covers over us like two corpses resting side by side in the morgue. On rare occasions, we made rudimentary love in the darkness. After it was done, we rolled apart and closed our eyes to forget our loneliness. It was as if we had lost our appetites for the other's skin, the other's spirit, and preferred sleep to cuddling.

It was ironic that the further we shifted apart as couple, the more we followed the rituals of husband and wife to the outside world. Almost every weekend, friends came by to be entertained in our new spacious accommodations. Endless socializing was a way for us to ensure that we did not spend too much time alone; otherwise, we were liable to argue. Our weekend parties were also a method to convince both ourselves and our friends that we were still functioning as a husband and wife.

After the conclusion of another weekend where friends had come to stay and I saw how the lights dimmed on Friede's face as soon as they were gone, I said to her, "You don't say you love me anymore; not the way you used to."

"What a foolish thing to say," she responded. "Do you think love is like the weather, where it can change by the hour? My love for you is no less strong just because I choose not to say it to you every second of the day."

There were moments, brief and beautiful when, Friede and I took a respite from our marital sturm und drang. These rapprochements started and ended without warning. Yet they were small graces that we appreciated as much as a sunny day after a month of rain. When they did occur, Friede generally suggested, "Let's not go into work today. Perhaps we can take a walk on the moors, and then for lunch find a cosy pub where we can spend the afternoon reading our books beside a nice warm fire."

The longer we remained at Tennyson Bungalow, the more we spent and the less we were able to save for our future or for an emergency. I lived in the moment that I knew was not going to last. Still, I savoured each Sunday when I was able to play crocket in our spacious backyard and afterwards smoke a Balkan Sobranie cigarette and drink a gin and tonic. It was, however, a lifestyle that I could not sustain as a workman in a confection factory. I knew that for us to remain in this house, I had to find a better paying job, or else we would be forced to move to another dingy squat in the nether regions of Halifax.

In May, I began to look around for another job. I enquired at factories stores and an office, but the only positions available for someone with my spotty educational background was hard labour, which promised little pay and no chance for advancement. It wasn't until I came across an advertisement for work at Humphries Carpets that I thought this might be a financially rewarding vocation.

It seemed a simple enough occupation: work on their looms to produce carpet runners. The wage was based upon one's production, so if I was fast and efficient, I'd make double what I earned at Macintosh's. I went over to their office and put my name down for the advertised job, and within a couple of days I was hired.

At Humphries, the work day was long and arduous. It was not uncommon to put in a twelve-hour day six days a week. I ran a giant weaving device that was able to spin multi-coloured spools of wool into carpet designs that imitated floral hand woven Indian carpets. The factory air was as heavy as butter, and the atmosphere was as polluted and inhospitable to human life as any industrialized plant in Northern England. Around me, a constant snow of wool particles, dust, and smog soiled my clothes and clogged my lungs.

I rarely took lunch but preferred to work through my breaks and attend to my giant loom, which threaded and knotted strong carpets destined for the stairwells of hotels, country inns, and new housing estates being built across our former colonies. At work, I kept to myself and made few friends.

On Fridays, I received my pay envelop and went to my bank to deposit my small remittance in the hopes that one day it would grow large enough that I could put a down payment on a house. Afterwards, I rode the bus to Tennyson Bungalow and over the weekend pretended with my wife that we were a married couple.

Chapter Nineteen:
Departure

In late July, the gardens at Tennyson Bungalow were vibrant hues of yellow, red, and lavender. Bird song was in the air, and it felt like we were finally going to have a summer to remember in the north. The brilliant colours, the warm days, and the resurgence of life were a sharp contrast to the rot that had invaded our marriage.

Both Friede and I knew that our marriage was pretty well bust, but we tried to keep the tempest of our emotions well hidden. Through the winter and spring, we drifted further apart, so by summer we were like two specs of land separated by a wide ocean. The only bridge we shared to each other was our mutual affection for our accommodations at Tennyson Bungalows. It was at least a refuge from Halifax, our uninspiring employment, and our disintegrating love affair; yet, our tenancy was to be cut short, and this added to our marital woes.

It was a midsummer Sunday morning when the owner asked me to walk with him in the garden. I thought that the request and his tone towards me were ominous, but I complied without question, hoping that my instincts were mistaken. The garden was bathed in the scent of blooming flowers and newly cut grass, and while we strolled together, dew drops clung to my leather shoes. The owner informed me that although he had enjoyed me and Friede as tenants, we had to move. As he put it, we were no longer necessary to maintain his mortgage payments. The owner had received a promotion at his work, which covered all of his expenses. "I am now general manager for my insurance company's regional office. I hope there are no hard feelings," he said and thanked me for being decent about the whole matter. This was no point in protesting or arguing with him because it was his house and his rules. I knew that the termination of our tenancy was going to be a bitter blow for Friede, as it was for me. At first, she was inconsolable. It was as if I had told her a close friend had died. For a long while, Friede succumbed to an intense grief over the loss of her sanctuary from Halifax and life in northern England. "I loved this house," she said in a distant and

163

melodious German accent. "In Hipperholme, I was relaxed, at ease with myself and this country."

By the time our annual holidays arrived in August, we had moved from Tennyson Bungalows and returned to the mean streets of central Halifax. There wasn't a lot of choice for us because housing was still scarce and our savings were not enough to afford living on our own. We moved into a terraced house and shared the rent with another a young couple who I had met through my work at Humphries.

The house was cramped, and although it was scrubbed clean, it was never free of insects, cobwebs, and the musty smell created by poor building materials. It was a depressing let down after spending months in virtual luxury in Hipperholme. I knew that both Friede and I would have preferred to live elsewhere, but that was just not possible at the time.

"We'll just have to make do," I said, more for my benefit than Friede's, "and hope by next year that things turn around for us."

"I don't think that will ever happen for us in Halifax," Friede remarked realistically. "No one wants you or me to be anything but worker bees."

Her words stung because they were true, and I tried to dismiss her protest with, "You are just too pessimistic sometimes."

"Look out our bedroom window and you tell me why shouldn't I be negative? It looks hopeless out there. The whole street," Friede said bitterly, "is overpopulated with families that look dirty and defeated. Even when you see them line up for church, their clothes look filthy, and it isn't their fault because I have come to realize that Britain has two types of people: the worker and the filthy rich."

"Change is coming," was all I could say in response. "It is just taking longer to reach the north, but change is coming because we hear about it every day on the wireless or on the newsreels. Everything will get better," I remarked in a lukewarm tone of voice.

Shortly afterwards, a transformation did occur, but it wasn't social or political; it was seasonal. One night, summer stole itself away in the darkness and was replaced by an austere autumn filled with wind, rain, and remorse. As the weather grew fouler, the civil discourse of our relationship went into hibernation.

164

By this juncture in our marriage, it no longer mattered to us if others witnessed our rows. We had given up caring about what anyone else thought about our relationship. We dispensed with arguing in whispers behind closed doors and brandished our displeasure publicly. We'd fight on the bus or walking down the street or in line to the cinema because our unhappiness with each other was as hard to conceal to the outside world as psoriasis. We argued through Guy Fawkes, Christmas, New Years, my birthday, Easter, and before bed. We argued pretty well from the start of 1950 until the summer came.

Sometime in late June, when the rains had stopped and Halifax looked refreshed, Friede and I ran out of anger, disappointment, and bitterness over our failed attempts to love one another. I surrendered to the inevitable conclusion that I had failed as a man. I had been unable to build a stable and prosperous life for our marriage to germinate and blossom. Whereas Friede came to the conclusion that her heart was not cut out for the life of an exile. She was no longer able to reconcile living in a foreign country and speaking a foreign tongue because her homesickness had maimed her spirit.

It only took a few sentences for me to know that the dance was over for me and Friede. Over tea and hard biscuits, Friede said in a quiet but resolved tone, "I can take no more of this. I want to go home."

"Home?" I asked, puzzled.

"Yes, I want to go home to Hamburg."

"Look," I said, "if you want to go on holidays, we are going to have to think of something closer by because we can't afford trips abroad at this moment."

She shook her head and said, "I think you and I are all washed up. It will be better for both of us to live apart and see what develops."

It was like a cold knife being plunged into my rib cage because I never thought that despite the pain and the miscommunication that it was ever going to end. I wasn't sure if I wanted it to end. I wasn't sure whether I wanted her to go. But hearing her say that she wanted to return to Germany signalled to me that our relationship as I knew it was over.

165

"Do you want to go for good?" I asked hesitantly.

"I am not sure," Friede said, and then her voice fell into a whisper as she completed her thought, "I need some time away from you and England. I want to return to my own country because I feel like a stranger here."

"I see," I said with little comprehension.

Friede's voice began to pitch in excitement as she continued to talk about Germany. "You know everything is different in Hamburg, since you were there. I have been told that people are really building for their future. Everything is being rebuilt, and there are so many new businesses that it really feels like Germany is on the move again. The people sense they are going to have a future within a democratic Europe. I don't see that happening anytime soon in England, do you?"

Even though I knew she was right, I grew angry at her and said, "Go on then, move back home, see if I care."

"Don't be like that; I know you are not happy with the way things are between us. It is better if we separated and try to remain friends at the very least."

"Friends?" I said with a tone of disgust.

"Why not?" she asked sadly. "We are both good people. Anyways, I still love you. But I'm not sure how that matters because we are sinking together and neither one of us is happy."

I threw up my hands and surrendered to her. "You can do whatever you want to do because I am not going to fight you anymore." Inside, I felt like a failure as a man, a husband, and as a human being. I thought, *Well, I am just like everyone else in my family: unlucky in love, cards, the whole bloody package.*

The following day, I set about making preparations for Friede's return to Germany. She was booked on an overnight ferry to Hamburg at the end of August. Before, she left I asked Friede to do one small favour for me and that was to lie to everyone we knew about the reason for her departure. "Tell them, you are going because your mother is unwell." She agreed but said, "I still don't know if I am ever going to come back to Britain."

On the day Friede's ship was scheduled to sail, I took her to Hull on an early morning regional bus. Friede's vessel was a converted fishing trawler that had room for twenty or so passengers. Since the trip to Hamburg was over twenty-four hours, I had reserved for her a single cabin with a shared WC. It was a spacious, above deck compartment. There was a large bed with a heavy wool blanket tightly tucked into it. Beside the bed was a comfortable chair to read in, while the room was encased in deep wood panelling.

When we entered her cabin, we brushed against each other, uncertain and reserved. Emotionally, we were as uncoordinated as when we first dated. I tried to act brave but looked more irritated and taciturn. I said things out of turn, in nervousness and sad anger, like a patient with a doctor who had just told him that the surgery wasn't successful and the cancer was growing.

"Don't be cross," she said.

"I'm not," I remarked and quickly changed the subject. "Your mother and friends will be glad to see you tomorrow morning. Are you sure you have enough money?"

"Yes, I don't need any more. You have been very kind."

If I am so kind, why are you leaving me? I wondered to myself.

"Well, at least you have a cabin to yourself."

"It is wonderful, thank you. You always get me nice things," she said.

On board the ship, I tried to read every line on her face, every physical gesture, every absence of touch as if it were an absolute sign, an indication of what lay concealed in her heart and her head. I needed to know like an angst ridden teenager if she had ever truly loved me or not or whether I had really loved her. It was dismal Kabuki theatre enacted by two inexperienced players.

Suddenly, there was a blast of steam from the engine, and people scurried down the corridors to go ashore. There was silence in her cabin, and we stared at each other haphazardly, unsure as to what to do next. She began to unpack her clothing. *Why did she insist on a single ticket and no return?* I pondered.

"Are you ever coming back?" I asked.

She looked up and said with little conviction, "I don't know; only time will tell."

Time for what? I wondered. *When will that date be? Will it ever arrive?* Somehow, I had failed and buggered my marriage up. *Smith,* I thought, *you drove her back to her homeland. You are a cock up, and a big, bloody fool.*

"Are you sure you have enough money, luv?"

"Yes," she said, tired and distracted, as if she were already in Germany, in Hamburg, amusing herself with friends in the *Planten und Blomen,* the city's botanical park where long walk ways were decorated on either side by exotic gardens.

"Right," I said with a laugh. "Best be off then; don't want them to think that I am a stowaway."

Friede smiled weakly at my joke. She then began to brush her short auburn hair back across her head in strong, agitated movements.

"Telegram me when you have arrived. Let me know when you have docked safe and sound," I set in a stern voice.

Friede set the brush on a table top and said, "A postcard will be more practical. I don't think the boat is in any danger of sinking."

"Goodbye, then."

"Yes, you must go," Friede said, and then moved to kiss me on the cheek. Her lips felt as cold as the sculpted marble lips of a saint's statue in church.

On shore, I watched the trawler beat its way out of the channel harbour and into the sea.   Standing on the pier, I looked at the trawler slipping away into the flat horizon. I was nauseous as I relived, second by second, the bust up of my marriage and witnessed it dissolving into the cold North Sea. My emotions mixed and formed into another nucleus, which combined in strong measure grief, anger, and shame. The power of all three emotions left me confused and gutted.

Chapter Twenty:
Exile

It was rather late in the day when I returned to Halifax from Hull. My bus dropped me off near the council building. Being Saturday, the streets were busy with workers enjoying the summer air and their day off. As I turned onto my street, I saw that the long rows of terraced homes were as active as an entrance to an ant colony. A group of noisy women traded gossip while taking down their laundry, which was strung out from the back of their flats to their bogs.

Nearby, children played games outside of their homes while from open windows their parents chastised them with hell and damnation, if they didn't get inside for their tea and pudding. It was always thus, I lamented, and looked skywards and saw that the horizon was cast in a hazy shade of red. It boded well for sailors but also told me that it was going to remain humid throughout the evening.

I opened up the door to our silent bed sit, and it smelled musty, old, and as worn out as I felt. Inside, it looked a shambles because earlier on Friede and I had scrambled to get to the port on time. *What does it matter?* I thought. *I'm not going to be having guests over for a long while. The place can look like a tip for all I care.* But my mood passed quickly from indifference to irritation at the mess.

I closed the door behind me and took off my suit jacket and hung it up neatly on a hanger and placed it into a cheap wardrobe. I pulled up my shirt sleeves and began to clean up the traces of my former married life. I scrubbed the dishes, swept the floor, and dusted the photos of me and Friede that had been taken in Germany. Afterwards, I sat in my chair by the coal fireplace and chain smoked. Somehow, I hoped the tobacco would singe the scent of Friede's perfume from the air, but no matter how much I smoked, I still felt traces of her fluttering about in the atmosphere.

What am I supposed to do now? I wondered. There was one thing I was certain about: I wasn't going to admit to anyone that Friede had left me. For the time being, I reasoned all that anybody needed to know was she had gone to Germany to visit her mother. It didn't seem like it was anyone's business but mine and Friede's whether our marriage was over or not. Besides, I was too proud to take pity from my friends about my messed up marriage, especially when all of them were no better off when it came to choosing a soul mate.

For a split second, it even crossed my mind to pack it all in - my job, my flat, my friends - and head for France. *Why not?* I thought. *I am still young, and there is nothing holding me here but bitter memories and lost illusions.* But the whim passed as quickly as it had entered my head. Somehow, going to France seemed tantamount to admitting that I was defeated by both love and life.

When sleep came that night, it brought me no relief; instead, I was teased by a lingering scent of Friede's body that rested in our sheets, and I was tortured by dreams about our former life together. In my subconscious brain, the history of our romance played out in disjointed parts and made me travel back through our romance after the war in Hamburg, our wedding in Germany, and then my return to Britain and demobilization.

It was a sweet relief for me when Monday morning came around and I was able to escape our flat and go back to work. Once I was inside Humphries' factory walls, I sighed at the respite from painful memories. I resumed work at my loom, and the miasma of dust, wool, noise, and heat pushed all thoughts or visions of Friede from my eye. The monotonous precision of my task ensured that my concentration was firmly fixed on controlling the giant unravelling coloured spools of thread that ran through metal prongs and stitched a predetermined pattern onto the carpets running through my loom.

During daytime, I was content because I consumed myself in my work, and that exhausted my body and mind. Yet, when darkness fell across our city like a death shroud, I was plagued with remorse, doubt, and self-recrimination because I was marooned alone with my emotions in our bedsit. I tried to dispel my gloomy outlook with bottles of ale, but it made my moods darker and my depression deeper.

Sometimes after work or on the weekends, I'd run into Irma and Roy on Commercial Street, and they'd inquire about Friede.

"She's just doing brilliant, but she says she misses me in spades. She can't wait to get back to Halifax."

"When is that?" Irma asked suspiciously.

170

"Don't know; it all depends on her mother's health. The poor dear really took a nasty turn, and with Friede as her only daughter, who else can properly tend to her?"

I received a post card from Friede two weeks after she left on the Goole Ferry for Hamburg. The message was short and unemotional and stated that she had arrived safe. It was signed "F", with no salutation of affection. *Well, to hell with you,* I thought and threw the card into a trash bin. That night, I drank way too much and woke with a horrible hangover, which increased my self-pity. So went many of my days: I worked my shift, returned home, and ate warmed up beans from a tin. Afterwards, I'd drink beer until I was ready to face an empty bed and a restless sleep.

I didn't think the contents of my life were going to change much in either the short term or long term. I grew increasingly afraid that I was going to end up like my father: estranged from the world, making do on crumbs while waiting for my end in a doss house. I avoided anything that reminded me about my former married life and ignored friends' requests for dinner, drinks, or walks. I explained my distance by saying that I was too busy at the mill to have a social life. Few bothered to broach the subject further because their own lives were complicated enough without having to unravel someone else's mess. I thought I was safe from anyone poking their nose into my business until one night as I returned from work I found Ingrid standing outside my front stoop.

"What are you doing in this neck of the woods?" I asked Ingrid, as I was very surprised to see anyone familiar near my home.

"I was out for a stroll, and somehow my feet led me here."

"Well, you better come in because the wind is picking up and I think there might be a storm. I'll fix you a cup a tea to get you warm." As we walked inside, I apologised and said, "I'm afraid it's a bit of a mess since Friede left for Germany."

"Don't bother me," replied Ingrid. "I am sure I have seen worse, especially with my husband Norman."

After I gave Ingrid that cup of tea, she was like a stray cat that showed up at my doorstep every time I returned home from work. I started to enjoy her visits because she flirted with me and massaged my ego with endless praise over my sensitivity and masculinity.

171

One evening after Ingrid prepared my supper, I was curious enough to ask her, "Doesn't Norman mind that you are over here?"

"He doesn't care about me, she said. "I can come and go like a dog as long as I leave him something to eat for his tea. My husband isn't much of a talker. He likes to keep things close to his chest, and all he asks of me is that I am obedient. He told me once if I was lonely he'd buy me a cat because he wasn't much for conversation. He likes things to be simple, and he doesn't want any fussing about."

"I see," I said, not entirely convinced that she was telling me the complete truth about Norman.

One night, Ingrid and I shared some drinks of gin and water, and after she grew tipsy she revealed to me that she was unhappy in her marriage.

"I've never been very lucky," she said. "I had a bad start in life, and my parents were rough people living in a rough time. When I met Norman, he wasn't a knight in shining armour; he was just a man that was decent enough not to be brutal to a girl. I didn't think I was ever going to do better than that in my life. I just had to find a man who didn't like to talk with his fists. He is not a bad man, but life in Halifax with Norman is like going to prison: I get food every day, a bed, but there is never going to be any sunshine in my life."

"I am sorry," I said. "Yorkshire is a very unforgiving climate to live in. We grin and bear it, but I think no one ever gets used to it. The only advice I can offer is: if you are unhappy, get out before it is too late because no one is going to thank you for staying."

"I bet you would," she said in a tone of voice that was reserved for lovers.

Desire trickled through my veins like water through a rusting pipe: at first in drips, then in a torrent. Ingrid must have sensed that I longed for her in that instant as much as she had pined for me. She leaned over to kiss me, and our lips met and brushed each other like a hummingbird flitting from one blossom to next. My lust didn't last, but instead evaporated as I remembered what kissing Friede meant to me. I gently pushed Ingrid away from me and said, "I am sorry, I can't do this; it just doesn't feel right."

"Why doesn't it?" she asked with a note of frustration in her voice. "You want me, and I want you...what is so difficult about that?"

172

"I'm married," I remarked lamely.

Ingrid laughed at me and said, "I don't know what your wife has to do with this. Everyone says that she has done a runner and is now in Germany. Any fool can see that your marriage is as kaput as mine."

"That is not entirely true," I said with a note of confusion in my voice. "She returned to Hamburg because her mother is ill and she hasn't seen her family in some time. It is completely natural for her to want to go back to her country for a visit."

"Do you honestly believe that?" Ingrid asked me.

"Yes," I said with utter conviction. My confusion over my feelings for Friede had cleared like a fever, and I knew I didn't want to kiss Ingrid again.

"We may have some problems in our marriage, but who doesn't? For a relationship to last forever it has always got to be mended and altered to adjust for changing circumstances; I am sure of that. We just became lost in the everyday world and forgot why we married in the first place."

Ingrid took me at my word but said that if I ever changed my mind, she would run away with me to the ends of the Earth. "You are a decent bloke, and they are hard to find these days."

Ingrid and I agreed that it was best for both of us if she stopped calling on me after work. For the next little while, my life returned to its normal routine of work, beer, and bed until I received a second post card from Friede. It said that she was headed for Berlin to search for her father and hoped that I was well.

A week later, another post card came from Friede, which had been sent from Berlin. *Can't find father or any trace of his family. Everything and everyone must have been incinerated by the war, and afterwards the Soviets. I am going back to Hamburg. Write me if you get the urge.*

Something told me that I had a very small window of opportunity with Friede to tell her how I truly felt about her. If I thought this marriage was worth saving, I had to let her know that I loved her, or else Friede was going to disappear from my world very quickly. It was now or never for me and Friede. Besides, I now knew that I wanted her back and was willing to fight to preserve my marriage. I wrote on the back of a post card, *Ich liebe dich, Harry,* and mailed it to her the following day.

Her answer arrived before the end of the week, but the response left me more mystified than satisfied. Friede wrote on her postcard: *We must speak. Call the telephone at my mother's apartment because I have too much to say and I can't explain it in a letter.*

It wasn't until the following day that I was able to place an overseas call to her at the central post office on Commercial Street. After the operator placed my call, I waited what seemed liked ages for the line to connect. When Friede answered the phone, the reception was poor and our words echoed as if we were speaking between a mountain and a valley. It didn't matter because I was happy just to hear her voice, no matter how distorted.

"I miss you," she said.

I was about to reply when a blip came over the line and indicated that I had to deposit some more coins into the box. I fed the phone and apologised, whereupon she said, "I've done a lot of thinking since I came back to Germany."

"Me, too," I said.

"Please hear me out, Harry; it is important," Friede continued. "I don't know if we are right for each other, and maybe we will always be the wrong size shoe when it comes to love and expectations. But I am certain of this: we are not going to make it together in Britain. Your destiny and my destiny will never be found in Britain. Your country is never going to give anyone like you a chance to get ahead and make a decent life for themselves. They don't want you to be any more successful than you are now because otherwise it would upset the established order and the way things have been done in Britain for generations."

I was about to dispute Friede's assertions but stopped because I knew she was making sense. I let her continue speaking.

"I am not saying it is not a beautiful country. It is a glorious country. I am not even saying that the people are bad in Britain because the ones I have met are the salt of the Earth. They are strong, resourceful, and full of humour and kindness. But we can't make a life out of songs about the last war and hope that we will get by. Besides, I think my life is worth more than just getting by, and I think yours is, too. We didn't survive a world war so that we could look forward to fried fish bits on Friday."

The phone blipped again, and I fed the coins into the machine as if I were paying the oracle of Delphi to tell me what portents lay ahead.

"What do you suggest?" I asked, feeling that there was no real solution to our dilemma.

"We have to move away from Britain," she said in a steadfast tone. "I will not live in that country if all we can expect is our life done on half rations."

"The rationing is coming to an end, slowly but surely," I said.

"It is not fast enough for me," said Friede, "because everywhere else in the world, people are prospering, but not in Britain."

"Well, I can't live in Germany," I said. "I love it there, but I don't think I'd be of much use to anyone there."

"You might be right," Friede agreed, "but I was thinking of somewhere new for both of us."

"Where?"

"Canada," she said with conviction. "It would be a new start for us in a new world. It is a country that wants a young couple like us to contribute and build a nation. In Canada we can have a future. In that new continent we won't have the weight of our pasts to drag us down into failure. I want to give our marriage a chance to grow in a country that is so immense, it can swallow all of our early disappointments and produce something wonderful."

Chapter Twenty-One:
The Empress of Australia

Not long after our telephone conversation, Friede returned to Britain with a greater sense of purpose and self-awareness. She went back to work at Macintosh's and was content knowing that her work on the chocolate wrapping assembly line was not permanent. Her friends noted that there was a perceptible change in Friede's personality. It was as if the emotional storms that had plagued her since she was a small girl were subsiding. This serenity was produced from the knowledge that for the first time in a long while, she believed that she had a future that had many wonders to offer her. Peace was also restored to heart because she understood that our marriage was not a failure and that although we loved each other, we had to strive to make our relationship function.

Friede's return to Britain and to me regenerated my ambition and my determination to create an interesting and rewarding life for us. I knew when I saw her disembark from her ship and wrap her arms around me that I would love her until time stopped for me; yet, I also realized that our love had altered since we had wed in the late summer of 1947. It had matured, and it had grown.

We now understood and celebrated the notion that we were individuals who had many differences. We had learned that those differences made us a stronger, not weaker partnership. From that point on, I would no longer doubt Friede's love or loyalty for me. It was as absolute as my love for her, and I hoped when we eventually reached our new life and land that it would flourish like a well-stocked fire to keep us safe.

It took close to three years before we finally were able to immigrate to Canada. Oddly, it didn't feel like an unendurable wait because in the meantime, we lived, we saved, and we enjoyed our time together. Our friendships with the other couples grew stronger, and new friendships were made with a Polish expat and his Belgian wife that were to have a profound influence on our life in Britain and abroad.

When the time came to book our passage, we went to a travel agency, near Saville Park. We dressed in our most fashionable clothes despite the fact that we were booking the cheapest fare.. The agent who prepared our sailing arrangements told us that the best ship he could recommend was the Empress of Australia, which was part of the Canadian Pacific fleet of steamships. It was considered a luxury liner despite the fact that the French navy had scuttled the ship during the war. "No fears," said the agent, "ships generally sink only once. So the Empress is as sound as the pound to get you to Montreal."

It didn't matter to me if we had to sail on a Corvette; I was ecstatic knowing that I was leaving Britain. "The Empress will do just fine for me and my wife," I said and paid him for our passage. The travel agent was a bit surprised when I gave him not only fresh new notes that I had withdrawn from the bank, but also included nine shillings and tuppence wrapped in a silk handkerchief. I looked at him and smiled and said, "This here is from my dad. He is dead, but before he died he wanted to help pay my fare to get out of this country. It might not be much to you, but to me, it is a king's ransom."

A month before the Empress was scheduled to sail from Liverpool to Montreal, I ran into my mother on the street. We hadn't spoken for a long while, but she told me, "A little bird told me that you are leaving Halifax."

"It is true, mum; Friede and I are going to Canada."

My mother was quiet, and then she spoke. "Make sure you don't drown in one of them lakes. I hear that in Canada, they be deep and cold. Its best you be gone, Harry, 'cause this country - like your old mum - is ready for the knackers." With that, my mother turned and resumed her day, and I was not sure whether her warning was said out of love or hatred.

It was a cold November night when The Empress of Australia slipped her moorings and sailed from the harbour in Liverpool. As the mighty ship began to glide away from the empty pier, Friede and I stood on the third class passengers' deck. The air was brisk and salty. We were bundled in heavy coats, our arms wrapped around each other's shoulders as we waved goodbye to the disappearing land of my birth.

In my imagination, I saw all the people who - whether living or dead - had influenced the course of my first thirty years bid me

178

farewell. The further we moved from land, the fainter were the echoes stirring from my past. The last one to leave me was comprised of words I thought my father might say to me: "It's time to make your mark, lad. Have a bloody good life for those of us who didn't." Soon, there was only silence from the shore, and the sound of the steam ship cutting through the sea towards the future.

The End

Books by the same Author:

1923: A Memoir
Hamburg 1947: A Place for the Heart to Kip
The Empress of Australia
The Barley Hole Chronicles
Harry's Last Stand

Printed in Great Britain
by Amazon